Situation Comedy 2

GW00634483

STUDIO SCRIPTS

Series editor: David Self

Working
The Boy with the Transistor Radio   *Willy Russell*
Good Prospects   *Charlie Stafford*
Strike   *Yolanda Casey*
George and Mildred   *Johnnie Mortimer and Brian Cooke*
Emmerdale Farm   *Douglas Watkinson*

City Life
Lies I, II   *Willy Russell*
Uncle Sangri   *Tom Hadaway*
Short Back and Sides, I, II   *Alan Plater*

Communities
Shove Up a Bit   *Gavin Blakeney*
Hush-a-Bye, Baby   *Gavin Blakeney*
Blind Eye   *Gavin Blakeney*
Old Fogey   *Julia Jones*
Nuts and Bolts   *Julia Jones*

Situation Comedy
The Liver Birds   *Carla Lane*
Happy Ever After   *John Chapman and Eric Merriman*
Rising Damp   *Eric Chappell*
Last of the Summer Wine   *Roy Clarke*
Going Straight   *Dick Clement and Ian la Frenais*

Love and Marriage
Gulpin   *Sheila Fay and Ken Jones*
First Date   *David Williams*
The Flight   *David Williams*
Just Love   *Leonard Kingston*
I Cried at your Wedding   *Madeline Sotheby*
Mum, Where are You?   *Eric Paice*

Power
A Little Patch of Ground   *Geoffrey Case*
The Protectors   *Cherry Potter*
Power   *Ludus*
My Sister's Eighteenth   *John McGrath*
Pantomime   *Derek Walcott*

School
Grange Hill   *Phil Redmond*
The Little Dissident   *George Baker*
Maids the Mad Shooter   *Farrukh Dhondy*
Headmaster   *John Challen*
Name in the Papers   *David Williams*

Situation Comedy 2

Edited by David Self

Hutchinson
London Melbourne Sydney Auckland Johannesburg

Hutchinson and Co. (Publishers) Ltd
An imprint of the Hutchinson Publishing Group
17-21 Conway Street, London W1P 6JD

Hutchinson Publishing Group (Australia) Pty Ltd
PO Box 496, 16-22 Church Street, Hawthorne, Melbourne, Victoria 3122

Hutchinson Group (NZ) Ltd
32-34 View Road, PO Box 40-086, Glenfield, Auckland 10

Hutchinson Group (SA) (Pty) Ltd
PO Box 337, Bergvlei 2012, South Africa

First published 1984
Selection, Introduction and Notes © David Self 1984

Set in Century Schoolbook

Printed and bound in Great Britain by
Anchor Brendon Ltd, Tiptree, Essex

British Library Cataloguing in Publication Data

Situation comedy 2. – (Studio scripts)

　1. Television plays　2. English drama (Comedy)

　I. Self, David　II. Series

　822'. 02'0817　PR1259.T4

ISBN 0 09 156481 6

Contents

Introduction
to the Scripts

Holiday camps, department stores, even disintegrating marriages and unemployment have all been the settings for successful television comedies, a type of programme which can perhaps best be defined as one which features a group of regular fictional characters, week by week, who behave in predictable ways in a given location or situation. The best attract huge audiences (rivalled only by those for the most popular 'soap operas' and for television screenings of major feature films). Consequently programme planners love to use situation comedies as 'building blocks' when they construct the schedules for a particular channel, often placing a favourite one early in an evening in the hope that viewers will then switch to that channel and stay with it for the rest of the evening.

Considering their popularity with viewers (and planners), it is no wonder that there are so many manifestations of the genre. However, quantity and popularity do not necessarily mean quality.

As with the previous collection of situation comedy scripts in this series, I have not simply selected representative scripts of the most popular series.

Some of these prove, on closer inspection, to be quite poorly written and rely heavily on the antics of a star comedian and the laughter of a studio audience to convince the viewer that he or she is watching something amusing. On the page, such scripts look distinctly thin. Others get their laughs by jokes or routines which are offensive to many and which seem distinctly unfunny in the cold light of day. (The question of what makes an acceptable comic target will be discussed later.) It has also seemed undesirable to include scripts which offer parts to very few readers or performers – a feature which might be most attractive to television accountants but which is less acceptable when the script is being considered for school or college use.

Consequently, in order to present scripts which will work well in the classroom or drama studio, those offered here are ones which have been written, in the main, for actors and actresses rather than for established comedians. It is hoped that a balance has been struck between those which have been memorable on television and those which will read well even if deprived of their visual effects.

It is also hoped that, besides giving enjoyment in their own right, these scripts will lead to a greater critical appreciation of situation comedy and of the characteristic features of their dialogue and structure.

Open All Hours
Open All Hours is set in and around a small corner shop in a town somewhere in Northern England. The central character (played by the very accomplished comic actor, Ronnie Barker) is the owner of the shop, Arkwright. His main interests in life are making as much profit as possible out of his customers, avoiding spending any money himself, and pursuing the buxom district nurse who lives opposite and to whom he is theoretically engaged. The other main character in the series is Granville, Arkwright's assistant and nephew (or, as we discover in this episode, half-nephew). The long-suffering Granville (played by David Jason) is much put upon by Arkwright and is also very shy. He comforts himself by imagining that his unknown father was a romantic Hungarian

and by decorating the bicycle on which he makes deliveries from the shop with a succession of motor-car accessories, dreaming of the van he wishes Arkwright would buy to replace the bicycle.

Roy Clarke, the author of the series, knows the setting well. His wife's father kept such a shop on Humberside, and Clarke remembers him opening the shop as early as five o'clock in the morning to serve customers on their way to work on an early shift.

Before becoming a full-time writer, Clarke was a teacher and his wife then ran another small corner shop in which he helped out in the evenings. However, he denies the suggestion that the series was inspired by this experience. 'It's written specially for Ronnie Barker.' In fact, Clarke had previously written a number of short comic character sketches for Ronnie Barker. In one, Barker played a prisoner. Out of this sketch grew the series, *Porridge* and *Going Straight*. Another character was the stuttering shopkeeper, Arkwright.

Some would suggest that it is wrong or cruel to use a stutter as a source of comedy, and that it is unacceptable to invite audiences to laugh at what is a form of handicap. Others, including some people who stammer or stutter, welcome the release that laughter brings. Another criticism that has been made of the series is that it is sexist in that Nurse Gladys Emmanuel is presented merely as a sex object. This she undoubtedly is in Arkwright's eyes, but it is a matter for debate whether we are being asked to laugh with Arkwright at her or at him. In practice, he never gets his way with her, and she frequently has the better of him. Indeed, much of the humour of the series stems from the scheming and miserly Arkwright getting his come-uppance.

Like many of the best situation comedies, *Open All Hours* gets its laughs from the interplay of character and is firmly rooted in realism, in this case the old-fashioned shop with such characteristic features as the till which constantly threatens to trap both Arkwright's and Granville's fingers.

The episode included here is from the second series and in it, besides the main characters with their usual preoccupations, we meet a succession of regular and occasional customers.

Only When I Laugh

Hospitals have frequently been used as settings by humorous writers but the situation comedy *Only When I Laugh* is unusual in that its central characters are not the doctors and nurses but the patients. In particular, they are the would-be upper-class Glover (played by Peter Bowles), the left-wing Figgis (James Bolam) and the slightly gormless Norman (deftly played by Christopher Strauli). In some episodes they are in conflict with one another, in others united against their doctor, Gordon Thorpe. The other regular character is a male nurse, Gupte. This is an interesting aspect of the series in that the nurse could so easily have been a 'stock' female character (perhaps either a sex object or 'dragon'). Gupte's Asian origins are never used as a basis for would-be humour, another distinctive aspect of this above-average comedy.

When it returned for a new series in Autumn 1981, the first episode (included in this collection) was reviewed in the magazine *Broadcast*, by W. Stephen Gilbert:

There are plenty of autumn sitcoms around. Best of those returning is Yorkshire Television's *Only When I Laugh*. Eric Chappell had the bright idea of a comedy about the devil making work for idle hands which gives plenty of opportunity for proper character development, credible situations and gags from confrontation rather than desperation. If his trio of male hospital patients seem unduly confined when nothing appears to be wrong with them, that's no matter. At least a hospital ward believably brings together those who would choose to be apart . . .

In this episode Chappell also shows he is ready to consider a serious question, such as the way television presents reality. So in others he has touched on unemployment and cuts in the health services. For example, in an episode called 'The Right Honourable Gentleman', a Thatcherite MP, concerned about rising Health Service costs, is admitted to the hospital for treatment. His refusal to sign a petition to save the hospital (to quote the *TV Times*) 'upsets other members of the ward, with hilarious results'.

Tradition has it that the independent television companies have been considerably less successful than the BBC in creating successful situation comedies. As one critic wrote in 1982:

The independent companies relentlessly seek the magic formula that will provide a situation comedy to emulate the institutions of the genre that the BBC disgorges with what appears to be effortless regularity. Poor loves, they still can't find it.

Yorkshire Television's *Only When I Laugh* disproves that rule, if rule it be.

Hancock's Half Hour

The radio series, *Hancock's Half Hour*, was one of the first genuine examples of situation comedy in Britain. It began in the early 1950s when two writers, Ray Galton and Alan Simpson (along with the comedian, Tony Hancock, for whom they had been writing a number of short comic sketches) set about persuading the BBC to let them do a half hour comedy programme without jokes as such but with the humour deriving from character and situation. As Alan Simpson has recorded, 'The format we were after was a storyline not split up by other acts. Just go straight the way through like a half hour play.' (Until then, the standard pattern for a comedy show was a series of comic sketches or solo turns, punctuated by a number of musical items.)

In the programmes, Tony Hancock's background and occupation were deliberately left vague. In some episodes he was an actor, in others a would-be local councillor, even a war veteran. The setting remained constant: Tony's home which was supposed to be in Railway Cuttings, East Cheam, where he was surrounded by a group of regular characters.

These included Sid James who was presented as a rather shady character from the criminal underworld, Bill Kerr who played a clueless Australian and Hattie Jacques who was variously Tony's housekeeper or girl-friend. Kenneth Williams played a variety of other characters.

When the programme transferred to television, Galton and Simpson's scripts concentrated on the relationship between Tony and Sid James and the other characters were replaced by ones played by 'straight' actors.

After a time, Hancock tired of what he thought appeared to be a double act and so he split up with Sid James. Only six programmes were made starring Hancock alone, but all of them became comedy classics and many people remember them with affection. In one, he was a radio 'ham' and in perhaps the most famous he was a blood donor. In the one selected for inclusion in this book, he is an actor with a role in a long-running radio soap opera, *The Bowmans*. The title makes it abundantly clear that this is a parody of *The Archers* and the character played by Tony (Joshua Merryweather) is not unlike the rustic Walter Gabriel in the real series. In this story, Joshua Merryweather is being written out of the serial, mainly because the producer of the radio programme and the rest of the cast can no longer tolerate the behaviour of 'Tony' at rehearsal.

This episode is interesting not only as a vintage script and one which showed the writers and Hancock at their best but also for the light it casts on another type of popular broadcasting, the soap opera. Just as the character Hancock is concerned about his position in the radio serial, so real-life actors in soap operas worry about their roles and images. Many may argue for contracts which, for example, guarantee them a stated number of appearances (and fees) a month.

Equally true-to-life is the 'death' of Joshua Merryweather which is treated as a real-life event by his fans in the story. Characters in actual soap operas are often believed in by some listeners and viewers who respond to their 'problems' with offers of help and messages of comfort. (See page 168.)

One question often debated when the *Hancock* programmes were first transmitted was how the character in the programmes compared with the real-life Tony Hancock. It has been answered at least in part by someone who knew him well, the television critic, Peter Black:

In real life Hancock was a serious, untidy, introspective person, sometimes marvellous fun to be with but too much of a worrier, a sensitive perfectionist, to enjoy his success. He never thought of himself as successful. He didn't like himself very much.

He believed he was unattractive and awkward. He identified with the quarry, never with the hunters. His huge earnings worried his sense of social justice. Too often his escape from anxieties and tensions was by way of the bottom of an upturned glass; the strings of girls, fast cars, yachts and racehorses were never for him, except as part of the comic world he and his writers had built. He had an unshakable sense of general doom.

After the six television programmes that Hancock made without Sid James he also parted company with his writers and started to look for new collaborators. Peter Black has recorded what happened.

Finally, he was unlucky that when he tried to move on he wasn't successful, partly because he never found writers who could light him up as splendidly as Galton and Simpson, partly because the drinking had begun to eat away at his performance. When I last saw him, in a one-man show from the Festival Hall, London, he seemed badgered, frustrated, as though his mind would no longer obey his will. He seemed to know that the drive to perfect his talent had gone too far wrong for him to be able to get it back. When he killed himself in Australia in 1968, he was only 44 but the news evoked more pity than shock.

His memorial is in the scripts . . . To read them years after their first performances is to rediscover with joy that Galton and Simpson when still in their early twenties were writing some of the most gloriously funny low comedy in the language.

A Fine Romance

If you are young and somewhat shy, you tend to suppose that your shyness is a problem of youth: only young people are shy of strangers. . . .

And when you are young you tend to think about when and if you will choose to marry someone and less about the question of whether anyone will marry you. But suppose you are in your mid-forties, still desperately shy of meeting new people and uncertain what to talk about when you do meet them and suppose, despite all your secret wishes, you are still not married. . . .

This is the 'situation' in *A Fine Romance*, a particularly delicate and delightful situation comedy by Bob Larbey, most of whose other work (such as *The Good Life*) has been written in conjunction with John Esmonde. Like *The Good Life*, *A Fine Romance* features two couples: Mike and Laura, and Helen and Phil. Helen and Phil are an attractive young married couple and Laura is Helen's older and plainer unmarried sister, who works as a freelance translator. Mike (who is also unmarried and is as shy as Laura) is a friend of Phil's and runs a rather shaky landscape gardening business. In the episode included in this book, the first of the series, Helen and Phil are giving a party and are also engaged in their regular pursuit of 'trying to find somebody' for Laura.

When the man they had thought of introducing to Laura cries off, Phil thinks of inviting Mike to the party and this episode shows us their first meeting.

All the cast are experienced and talented serious actors

though equally gifted in presenting comedy. Michael Williams and Judi Dench (well known for their work with the Royal Shakespeare Company) play Mike and Laura, and Susan Penhaligon and Richard Warwick play Helen and Phil. Their contribution to the series was noted by W. Stephen Gilbert in the magazine *Broadcast*:

Welcoming Judi Dench and Michael Williams to the genre is a great pleasure and they speak the lines as if from their own heads. So many of their exchanges exemplify the relationship – 'You don't have to impress me, you know,' she snaps. 'I'm not. That's the trouble,' he sighs. He's the endearing wimp, she's the spirited melancholic. The joke is that they absolutely suit each other but find it excruciatingly difficult to yield to it. Such problems are very real, which is unusual in sitcom, and the escapades – a lost contact lens, unwelcome assistance, the doomed dinner – are real too.

Fundamentally, it's about image and self-image, a good subject amusingly explored and played expertly enough for a little to go a long way. Good support too from Susan Penhaligon, so accomplished that Dench suffers all the more, from Richard Warwick who always says the wrong thing.

The early series were produced and directed with subtlety and wit by James Cellan-Jones, known mainly for his work in television drama. Equally distinguished are Bob Larbey's scripts with their economic style and gentle understatement.

Yes Minister

It is often suggested that, for a situation comedy to be successful, the 'situation' must be one that is immediately recognizable and familiar to the viewer, but few of the many enthusiastic and regular viewers of *Yes Minister* can have much firsthand knowledge of a Minister of the Crown's office in Whitehall.

The very first episode explained the situation. For some years Jim Hacker had been MP for the marginal (and of course imaginary) constituency of Birmingham East, and also a 'shadow minister'. That is to say, Hacker's party (it is never specified of which one he is a member) had been in Opposition and he had been its spokesman in the House of Commons on a particular subject. There had then been a general election and Hacker's party was returned to power. The Prime Minister (whose sex is never identified) invited Hacker to become a minister – not one of the important ones such as Chancellor of the Exchequer but (another fictional name) the Minister for Administrative Affairs.

This first episode went on to show us Hacker arriving at the Ministry and meeting the permanent staff there, two of whom figure prominently in each future episode.

These are Sir Humphrey Appleby, the senior civil servant who runs the ministry, and Bernard Woolley, the official whose job it is to be an assistant to whoever is the Minister. The 'situation' of the series therefore is the constant battle as to who is in charge: Jim Hacker, the politician who is there so long as the Prime Minister wishes – or until he loses his seat in Parliament or until his party loses an election; or Sir Humphrey who is officially the politician's servant but who has a secure (and very well-paid job) and who knows far more about the department than does Hacker.

When *Yes Minister* returned for a second series in 1981, Michael White, Parliamentary Correspondent of the *Guardian* newspaper described some of the background to the series in an article in *Radio Times*:

It is just a year since this unlikely idea for a hit comedy series – the power struggle between Ministers and Civil Servants, surely not? – first reached our screens (after hanging around until the delayed General Election was over). But the Antony Jay–Jonathan Lynn creation has rapidly acquired cult status, not least among its victims. Mrs Thatcher sent out for a complete set of video recordings and declared it to be one of her favourite programmes. Former Labour Cabinet Ministers have been heard to describe it as 'fantastically true to life'.

As for the mandarins of Whitehall themselves, they discuss it during scholarly seminars and, when confronted with an awkward letter, have been known to murmur: 'Now, what would Sir Humphrey do about this?'

Other sources of inspiration for the series have been noted by its writers. Antony Jay acknowledges its debt to a very different situation comedy:

I was watching *Steptoe and Son* and it came to me: that lovely structure which has two people bound together and needing each other, but having different motivations and being forced apart. There is no comedy about people being forced apart unless there is an equal force holding them together. That's why husband-and-wife comedies are so powerful.

Jonathan Lynn suggests another source:

We are also following one of the few other situation-comedy formulas, the one about the servant who is cleverer than his master, like Jeeves and Bertie Wooster.

Some people have suggested that *Yes Minister* is an important television series because it shows us what really does go on in government and Whitehall. There is no doubt that it is very realistic in its details and revealing (and indeed frightening) in the way it shows how both civil servants and politicians are interested in not so much the good of the nation as their own immediate interests. However, some critics have suggested (with reason) that the series is not a stunning revelation of wickedness in high places but a rather cosy nod of approval to such activities. In one episode, Hacker may be the hero; in the next it is Sir Humphrey who is triumphant. More often, they connive in a course of action which is in their mutual interests.

Whether you believe the series attacks or supports 'the system', it remains a fact that it is beautifully written and acted with style by Paul Eddington as the MP, Nigel

Hawthorne as Sir Humphrey and Derek Fowlds as Bernard Woolley.

The script selected for this collection raises a number of interesting debating points about conservation, action groups and the whole question of just how much about what goes on in government the public has 'The Right to Know'.

The Writers

Eric Chappell

Eric Chappell's first play was *The Banana Box* which was presented at Hampstead Theatre Club for a Sunday night performance in November 1970 and has subsequently been staged at the Phoenix Theatre, Leicester; the Theatre Royal, Newcastle; and Oxford Playhouse, prior to a successful West End run. His first situation comedy, *Rising Damp*, was based on this play.

Since then he has had a number of his plays televised, including *The Spanish Dancers* and *We're Strangers Here* (now also a stage play). He also wrote the television serial *The Squirrels*, and the very successful and popular series *Only When I Laugh*. A number of his plays have also been presented on radio, and his other situation comedies have been *The Misfits* and *The Bounder* (which, like *Only When I Laugh*, starred Peter Bowles).

Roy Clarke

Before turning to full-time writing (in 1968), Roy Clarke had a very varied career including teaching in a secondary modern school, two years with a county police force and odd jobs as door-to-door salesman, office clerk and part-time taxi driver.

His first work was for radio: two thriller serials (both produced by Alan Ayckbourn) and a single play called *The

World of Miss Edwina Finch's Cat. His first work for television was an episode of *The Trouble-Shooters* for BBC Television. He has written several other single plays and series including *Falling Star* (1970), *The Regulars* (1973), *The Bass Player and the Blonde* (1977), and *Flickers* (1980).

It was in 1972 that he first turned his attention to situation comedy, and a pilot episode for *Last of the Summer Wine* was transmitted in 1973. He also wrote a great deal of material for Ronnie Barker between 1972 and 1975 including *Open All Hours.* Since then he has written the series *Rosie* and *Potter.*

Ray Galton and Alan Simpson

Ray Galton and Alan Simpson first met in 1948 when they were in the same sanitorium, undergoing treatment for tuberculosis. While there, they wrote comedy scripts for the hospital radio service and, after leaving hospital, wrote for a church concert party. By 1951 they were writing professionally for BBC Radio and for such performers as Frankie Howerd, Peter Sellers and Eric Sykes. It was at this time that they met Tony Hancock. The first series of *Hancock's Half Hour* was broadcast in 1954. The show ran on radio for five years and consisted of 101 episodes. Galton and Simpson also scripted sixty-three episodes for television between 1956 and 1961. After their partnership with Hancock ended, they wrote *Comedy Playhouse* for BBC Television, out of which grew the extremely popular *Steptoe and Son.* This has been a great success in many countries, including the United States where it is known as *Sandford and Son.* They have also written a number of film scripts, for the theatre and also *The Galton and Simpson Playhouse* for Yorkshire Television.

Bob Larbey

Bob Larbey was born in South London and first met his writing partner, John Esmonde, at school. It was after their national service that they met again and began their joint writing career. Their first big success was a series for London Weekend Television, *Please Sir*, which was followed by its 'spin-off', *The Fenn Street Gang*. They have written several other series together, including *Get Some In* and *Don't Rock the Boat* for Thames Television and *The Good Life* and *The Other One* for BBC Television. *A Fine Romance* was Bob Larbey's first solo venture and an immediate success when it was first shown in 1981. It has won the Broadcasting Press Guild Award for the Best Comedy of the Year.

Antony Jay and Jonathan Lynn

Antony Jay was a BBC-tv producer for ten years, leaving in 1964 to become a writer and communications consultant. As director and chairman of a company called Video Arts, he has written and produced many comic films designed to train managers. Jonathan Lynn became an actor on leaving Cambridge, studied in New York, has been in many West End successes and appeared regularly on television, including series such as *The Liver Birds* and *Doctor in the House*. He has been artistic director of the Cambridge Theatre Company and directed many other productions in London. As well as writing three series of the award-winning *Yes Minister* with Antony Jay, he has written many other situation comedies, a novel and film scripts.

Notes on Using the Scripts

The most informal classroom reading of a playscript is helped by rehearsal. Even a very experienced professional actor prefers to look over his part before a first reading in front of his colleagues. In the classroom therefore, those who will be reading should be given time to look over their lines: to make sure that they know when to pause, when to 'interrupt' the previous speech, and to work out the changing mood of their character before they are asked to read aloud.

It is much easier to read to a group from the front of a traditional classroom, and from a standing position or a position where you can be seen by your audience. It may be helpful to appoint a 'director' who will decide the location of various settings and rehearse the actors in basic movements, checking that they know when and where to enter and exit.

Note that it is possible for a group to break up into smaller groups, and for each of these to rehearse its own part of the script, or its own interpretation. These groups can then present their parts or versions in turn to the whole class.

Even if you have seen the television production of any of the shows, resist the temptation to copy the screen version. Study the scripts and work out your own interpretations.

In preparing the scripts for inclusion in this book, some of the film and studio directions have been modified so that these directions (along with scene titles and descriptions of settings) can be read aloud by a narrator. In a classroom presentation, it is helpful if he or she is in view of the 'audience' but away from the acting area.

A television script will read just as fluently in the classroom as will any other kind of play; but don't forget that it was conceived in visual terms. Discuss (as the original director must have done) where and how each scene should be 'shot' to realize the author's intentions.

Work out which scenes were recorded on a studio set, and for which scenes it was necessary to go filming on location.

You could also adapt and then tape-record them to see how effective your reading has been.

The following points may be of help when recording:

(a) Practise with your microphone to discover from how wide an angle it can pick up sound clearly.

(b) Even the best microphone cannot produce a good recording over a long distance from the sound source. For speech, it should be 30-40 centimetres from the mouth. (Those readers with stronger voices can obviously be further away than those who do not project so well.)

(c) It is much easier to record a play with actors standing rather than sitting. (They can easily tiptoe away when not involved in a dialogue, and so allow those who are speaking to stand in the best positions.)

(d) Do not hold the script between mouth and microphone, and avoid rustling pages.

(e) Rooms with bare walls produce a lot of echo. Unless an echo effect is required (for scenes set in a hospital corridor for example) if possible use a carpeted, curtained room for recording.

(f) Sound effects are important in any taped play. Don't worry about including every sound, but concentrate on those background noises which suggest location (for example, street noises, etc.) and sounds which indicate the arrival or

departure of a character. Avoid clumsy and accidentally comic sounds (like artificial footsteps) which can clutter or confuse the much more important dialogue.

(g)   Gently fading out the very last few words or sounds of a scene and fading in the first sounds of a new scene will suggest a transition from one scene to another.

Acknowledgements

For permission to publish the plays in this volume, the editor and publishers are grateful to the following authors and their agents:

Roy Clarke and Sheila Lemon Ltd (17 Elverton Street, London SW1) for *Open All Hours*; Eric Chappell and Bryan Drew Ltd (Quadrant House, 80-82 Regent Street, London W1) for *Only When I Laugh*; Ray Galton, Alan Simpson and Tessa Le Bars Management (18 Queen Anne Street, London W1) for *Hancock's Half Hour*; Bob Larbey and Sheila Lemon Ltd for *A Fine Romance*; Jonathan Lynn, Antony Jay and Jan van Loewen Ltd (21 Kingly Street, London W1) for *Yes Minister*.

No performance of these plays, either amateur or professional may be given unless a licence has been obtained. Applications should be addressed to the authors' agents.

Ronnie Barker as Arkwright, David Jason as Granville and Lynda Baron as Nurse Gladys in Open All Hours. (BBC copyright)

Open All Hours
Series 2, episode 3
Roy Clarke

First shown on BBC-1 on 15 March 1981 (produced by Sydney Lotterby)

Characters

Arkwright, a shopkeeper
Granville, his assistant and nephew
Nurse Gladys Emmanuel, a district nurse
Mrs Blewitt, a customer
Mavis, another customer
Workman
A pimply youth
A van driver
Mr Glastonbury ⎫
Mr Rafftree ⎬ *(non-speaking customers)*
Mr Ellis ⎭

Open All Hours

---

1 Outside Arkwright's shop

Granville *is outside, cleaning the shop window.* **Arkwright** *comes out for a breath of fresh air, and* **Granville** *pushes gruffly past him and goes into the shop, without saying a word.*

Arkwright: [*To himself*] I'm getting worried about Granville. He's at a f-funny age. Oh that's nice – I'm stuttering when I'm only thinking now!

[*He checks the window, and sees a sign saying 'Help – I am being held a prisoner against my will'* **Granville's** *face appears above this*]

Arkwright: Granville – f-fetch your cloth!

2 Inside the shop

It is dawn. The milkfloat rattles past outside. **Granville** *turns the light on in the shop and walks to the shop door. His mouth opens in a yawn as he changes the 'Closed' sign to 'Open'.* **Arkwright** *comes in, looking freshly shaved, bright-eyed and ready for action. He surveys his little kingdom and rubs his hands together briskly.*

Granville: What do you always do that for?

Arkwright: What for?

Granville: This.

[*He rubs his hands together*]

Arkwright: That's the shopkeeper's chafe. We do it for luck to remind ourselves how fortunate we are not to be grasshoppers. Because that poor creature, in order to make a similar noise, has to rub his hind legs together. [*He winces at the idea*] If shopkeepers had to do that, just imagine what that would do to their overheads.

Granville: Every morning. This. [*He rubs his hands together again*] You'll be doing it once too often. Your hands will burst into flames.

Arkwright: Do I detect in the heart of that little embryo shopkeeper an air of b-belligerence?

Granville: [*Crossing to the shop door to undo its many bolts*] Yes. You do detect an air of b-belligerence. [*Angrily*] How many more bolts are you going to put on here?

Arkwright: Who's got out of bed the wrong side, then?

Granville: There is no right side at this time in the morning.

Arkwright: You should get to bed at night.

Granville: It's nine o'clock before we close. I got out for an hour, it's midnight before I can turn round.

Arkwright: That's what you do, is it? T-turning round. It sounds very dubious to me. There'll be no good come of young couples out at midnight t-turning round.

Granville: I don't know what we have to open at this time for. I was dreaming I was cruising the main drag.

Arkwright: Where?

Granville: Las Vegas.

Arkwright: I thought you meant Huddersfield.

Granville: Looking for a hot fruit machine.

Arkwright: You want a hot fruit machine. There's one in the kitchen.

Granville: Where?

Arkwright: The gas oven. When the early morning rush is over you can make us an apple pie.

Granville: Early morning rush? We get six blokes and a sheepdog.

Arkwright: Sometimes all at once. G-get ready. They'll be in in a minute with no time to spare to catch that first bus. [*Examining his stock of biscuits*] Oh dear, we've got too many fig biscuits. I want you to start pushing fig biscuits.

Granville: Me own uncle gets me up before dawn just to open a door for somebody's sheepdog!

[*The door opens, and a dog enters with a basket in its mouth*]

Arkwright: Well come on – see what he wants

[**Granville** *takes a note from the basket and reads it*]

Granville: Good-morning sir – what can I do for you? Large tin of baked beans, packet of firelighters.

Arkwright: No fig biscuits?

Granville: [*To the dog*] Fig biscuits, sir? ... No fig biscuits.

[**Granville** *loads the goods into the dog's basket. He opens the door for it and it goes out*]

Arkwright: And keep your hind leg off the b-brushes and b-brooms!

Granville: [*Watching the dog out of the door*] He's certainly obedient. Didn't go near them. He did it on the seed display-stand.

Arkwright: Oh heck! I hope they don't start g-germinating.

Granville: Doesn't it ever worry you that life's passing us by while we're stuck here serving incontinent dogs?

Arkwright: No, it doesn't worry me. Not as long as they're paying cash. Get that money in the till.

Granville: [*Crossing to the counter*] Why don't you put it in?

Arkwright: It'll w-wake you up.

[**Granville** *moves reluctantly to the till but he hesitates*]

Arkwright: Go on then. G-get it in.

[**Granville** *picks at the spring carefully*]

Arkwright: Oh give it here, you big girl's blouse!

[**Arkwright** *snatches the note and inserts it swiftly in the till, narrowly avoiding the spring*]

Granville: I'm going to open that one day and it's going to be full of loose fingers.

Arkwright: Get off.

[*He rubs his hands together again*]

Granville: There you go again. Make the most of it, while you've still got some fingers left.

[*He imitates the action*]

Arkwright: There's n-no need for you to do it.

Granville: [*Imitating him*] There's n-no need for you to do it.

Arkwright: I have to keep these hands at room temperature

— in case they're ever required to decant any of the sp-sparkling vintage full-bodied white, known locally as n-nurse Gladys Emmanuel.

Granville: I don't know why you don't give that up as a bad job. She's never going to marry you.

Arkwright: She might – we're engaged, why shouldn't she?

Granville: Because your interests aren't broad enough.

Arkwright: Listen, she's broad enough for both of us.

Granville: She wants more from life than somebody who knows how to calculate percentages in his head.

Arkwright: It's just a knack. Something I've been knackered with since birth.

Granville: Get up. Here they come. Hot foot for the first bus.

[*They just have time to take up their positions before the sleepy workmen arrive and make a bee-line for their cigarettes, which* **Arkwright** *has lined up on the counter. The men are all coughing heavily*]

Arkwright: Morning, Mr Glastonbury. Here you go then. Twenty for you. Mr Rafftree. Thank you. Whose hand is this? Oh it's your's, Mr Ellis. I thought, 'Hallo, there's some posh stranger wearing gloves' – it must be nicotine.

[**Granville** *is kept busy trying to cover items of stock from the effects of their coughing*]

Arkwright: That's it. Just throw your paper on the floor. My assistant here will sweep everything up when you've gone. And if he f-finds a pair o'lungs the owner can collect them anytime up to nine o'clock. Granville – they're on the move. Hold that door open, Granville. Say good-morning to your customers.

[**Granville** *holds the door open*]

Granville: Morning . . . [*He nods to them as they pass out of the shop and covers his face to avoid their coughing. He sighs with relief when they've all gone*] We'd have less fumes and racket if we brought the bus in here and let that lot wait outside.

[*He starts uncovering the stock*]

Arkwright: There's a lot of effort goes into coughing like that. If there was some way of harnessing that energy I could heat this place for the rest of the week.

Granville: And if it was free you'd maybe let me have some heat in my bedroom – instead of living up there among all the perishables you haven't got room for in the cold store.

Arkwright: Listen, the last thing a young man needs at your tricky age is a w-warm bedroom. Do you realize how many unnatural practices are d-directly attributable to central heating? And talking of eating – let's get some breakfast.

Granville: That's an unnatural practice. Eating at this time of the morning – in the middle of the night.

[*He goes to the kitchen*]

Arkwright: I wonder what happened to Mr Harris – I hope he hasn't given up coughing for Lent.

3   The kitchen

Arkwright *is reading his newspaper in an armchair, and* **Granville** *is making a pie.* **Arkwright** *turns a page.*

Arkwright: Oh dear. Tut, tut, tut. Terrible.

Granville: What is?

Arkwright: This page.

Granville: What page?

Arkwright: The page with your fingermarks all over it.

Granville: Oh, that page.

Arkwright: This newspaper's full of young ladies' upper attributes.

Granville: Why don't you change it, if you don't like it? For something with more substance.

Arkwright: I wouldn't want to see a lot more substance than this. Look at that – she's got more front than Eastbourne.

Granville: You ought to take a serious newspaper. Prove to Nurse Gladys you've got other interests.

Arkwright: Listen – she's never let me prove me f-first interest yet.

[*The shop bell rings, and* **Arkwright** *goes through to the shop*]

Granville: Can you get that? My hands are all floury.

[*He turns round, but* **Arkwright** *has already gone*]

Granville: Hey – it's sharpened his reflexes up, nearly missing that customer last week.

4   Inside the shop

Mrs Blewitt *stands grimly and uncompromisingly in the middle of the shop as* **Arkwright** *enters.*

Arkwright: Good-morning, Mrs Blewitt.

Mrs Blewitt: Is it? You wouldn't think so if you had to run about after *him*. Sixty-four years old and he still can't keep a button on his shirts! I'll have a tin of my polish and a bottle of bleach.

Arkwright:　Another tin of polish, Mrs Blewitt?

Mrs Blewitt:　Aye. They don't go very far.

Arkwright:　You must have a n-nice clean place there to be miserable in.

Mrs Blewitt:　You'd be miserable if you lived up with *him*. If he's not under me feet he's down there at that British Legion Club trying to drink his way back through the Second World War! I wouldn't mind, but he only got as far as Aldershot.

Arkwright:　There's just you and him, now the kids have gone?

Mrs Blewitt:　More's the pity. He never was any help.

Arkwright:　How many kids was it?

Mrs Blewitt:　Seven.

Arkwright:　Oh dear. How much help do you want? At least it explains some of them missing buttons.

Mrs Blewitt:　Is that a strong bleach?

Arkwright:　Strong, Mrs Blewitt? It's vicious. You can hear it s-seething in the bottle on a still night.

[*She looks round for eavesdroppers*]

Mrs Blewitt:　You'll not have seen Mrs Moffat?

Arkwright:　Not this morning, no.

Mrs Blewitt:　Nor yesterday?

Arkwright:　No.

Mrs Blewitt:　She's been seen.

Arkwright:　Has she?

Mrs Blewitt:　In Chesterfield.

Arkwright: Not a lot to boast about, but - er - not exactly illegal, is it?

Mrs Blewitt: That's where *he* lives.

Arkwright: He? Who?

Mrs Blewitt: Her fancy man. In Chesterfield.

Arkwright: Her f-fa- Her f-fa- Her f- boyfriend?

Mrs Blewitt: Yes. [*She looks round and then bends to confide in* **Arkwright**] She's had him for years.

Arkwright: She seemed such a quiet little woman.

Mrs Blewitt: They're the worst.

Arkwright: Mind you, that's true . . . I should have known all along. She never did buy any.

Mrs Blewitt: What? Buy any what?

Arkwright: [*holding up a pack of biscuits*] Not a s-single pack of these fig biscuits which at reduced prices represent a m-most economical supplement to the household diet.

Mrs Blewitt: Fig biscuits?

Arkwright: The very same. The chaste housewife's indicator – the fig biscuit.

Mrs Blewitt: What's so special about fig biscuits?

Arkwright: Nothing which the customer would notice, I suppose. [*He fondles the pack of biscuits*] It takes a lifetime of shopkeeper's experience to sp-spot a connection like that.

Mrs Blewitt: Connection like what?

Arkwright: The fig connection – the connection between respectable womanhood and the fig biscuit. D-don't ask me to explain it. All I can tell you is, Mrs Blewitt, you show me an order without a fig biscuit and I'll show you a housewife of doubtful moral r-rectitude. Now let me see, that was a bottle of bleach and a tin of polish.

Mrs Blewitt: And a packet of fig biscuits.

Arkwright: And a packet of fig biscuits.

5   The street outside the shop

Nurse Gladys *is loading up her Morris Minor as* **Arkwright** *ushers* **Mrs Blewitt** *from the shop. His eyes light up at the sight of the nurse and he wanders over.*

Nurse: Not too close, Arkwright. At this time of the morning I bruise easily.

Arkwright: N-Nurse Gladys Emmanuel. For whom I have only the gentlest intentions.

Nurse: The only time you go gentle is when you're spending anything. I'm going to work.

Arkwright: Oh, I hate to think where them hands will have been by the time you get back home. If you're going to g-grab me, you better do it now, while your fingers are still fresh.

Nurse: Out of the way, silly beggar. You get worse.

Arkwright: Allow me to assist you into your vehicle.

Nurse: No thank you.

Arkwright: Go on Gladys – let me give you a helping hand where I need it most.

Nurse: You'll do nothing of the kind. Clear off.

Arkwright: If you've got to handle anything n-nasty wear your gloves.

[**Nurse Gladys** *drives off*]

6   Inside the shop

Granville *is wheeling the shop bike through, laden with deliveries.*

Granville: This shop bike's useless – it's totally clapped out.

Arkwright: Oh dear, you're just like your mother.

Granville: That's a nice thing to say about your own sister.

Arkwright: Well, half-sister really. We often used to wonder which half. You see me f-father married again. He never got anything right the first time.

Granville: You're going to have to have this damned bike fixed.

Arkwright: Just j-jiggle it a bit.

Granville: I spend half me life just j-jiggling it a bit.

Arkwright: Your mother was wild and rebellious. Come on, get out.

Granville: I can't even remember what she looked like.

Arkwright: Big, beautiful, buxom. You must take after your father.

Granville: What was he like?

Arkwright: Lightning. Now get off and take them orders out. And d-don't be all day.

Granville: Do you think he was Hungarian? She must have loved him to keep his identity secret like she did.

Arkwright: Maybe she couldn't pronounce it.

Granville: Just think – if she hadn't met him I wouldn't a been here.

Arkwright: You shouldn't be here now. Come on. You should be out delivering them orders.

Granville: It makes you think, doesn't it? What a narrow line there is between who gets born and who doesn't get born. I could have been one of the nameless unborn.

Arkwright: Don't worry, I would have thought of something to call you.

[**Granville** *leaves, nearly knocking over a* **Workman** *who is coming in*]

Workman: Who's that stupid young twonk?

Arkwright: Some Hungarian.

7   The street

Granville *is pedalling the shop bike, which has acquired a few motor accessories. He approaches a* **Pimply Youth** *in greasy overalls, working on his Spitfire, head under the bonnet.*

Granville *presses a button which sounds off a musical motor horn, causing the* **Youth** *to jump and crack his head on the bonnet.*

Granville *pedals on, grinning.*

8   Inside the shop

Arkwright *is behind the counter serving a harrassed-looking woman,* **Mavis***. She has one or two things already in a little pile on the counter. She looks round the shelves in a great quandary of indecision.* **Arkwright** *waits alertly for her next instruction.*

Mavis: I better have a tin of soup.

Arkwright: One tin of soup, thank you Mavis. L-large or small?

Mavis: Large.

[*He moves accordingly*]

Mavis: No. Small.

[*He moves to another shelf*]

Arkwright: Oxtail? Mulli-ga-mamul-ma-mulli. Mulligatat, a Mulliga Tomato?

[**Mavis** *considers the options*]

Mavis: Oxtail.
Arkwright: Oxtail.

[*He takes a tin down from the shelf*]

Mavis: No, tomato.

[*He puts it back and gets another one. He pauses, ready for her to change her mind again*]

Arkwright: T-tomato?
Mavis: Yes.

[**Arkwright** *walks towards the far corner of the shop*]

Mavis: Unless you've got . . . Scotch Broth.
Arkwright: Scotch broth? That's very exotic, Mavis. I haven't got a small tin, I've only got a large tin.

[*He plonks one down on the counter, and she studies it*]

Mavis: Oh! [*She is in a real dilemma now*]

Arkwright: I can't cut it in half, Mavis. I'll t-tell you what. Take the large one and I'll charge you for two small ones.

[*She smiles happily*]

Mavis: Oh thank you, Mr Arkwright. I don't know whether I ought to take a tin of luncheon meat.
Arkwright: Is it on the list?
Mavis: Yes. [**Arkwright** *plonks a tin on the counter*] But I crossed it out.

[*He puts a cross on the tin*]

Arkwright: And 23p for my shoe leather.

9   The street outside the shop

Granville, *pedalling gamely, is startled into a speedy wobble by the musical horn of a beaten up old Spitfire driven by the* **pimply youth** *in mechanic's overalls, who gives* **Granville** *a thumb-to-nose sign as he passes.*

Pimply youth: You're a lovely mover, Granville.

[**Granville** *replies by flapping his hands by his ears, loses control and narrowly avoids running into the back of a van which is making a delivery at the shop.*

The **Driver** *has his back to* **Granville** *while sorting out his trays. He is talking to* **Arkwright,** *who stands nearby and who can see* **Granville's** *approach, and the attempts* **Granville** *is making to brake*]

Driver: We've all got to move with the times. What you really ought to try, Mister Arkwright ... [**Arkwright** *winces in anticipation of the collision*] is some of our new inspirational ... [**Granville's** *front wheel slides between the* **driver's** *legs, sending his voice up an octave*] toilet rolls.

10   Inside the shop

Arkwright *is behind the counter.* **Granville** *enters with a sack.*

Granville: You don't care about me.

Arkwright: I feed you and clothe you, don't I?

Granville: You send me out dressed like this on that antique shop bike.

Arkwright: It's a g-great little machine, is that.

Granville: It's not a lot o'good for my sporting image though, is it? Other people my age have little sports cars.

Arkwright: Listen, little sport, you did enough damage to that van driver with your bike.

Granville: You don't care about me.

Arkwright: You were going too fast on that bike.

Granville: It's the only excitement I've got in me life, speed.

Arkwright: If I hadn't been there, you'd have been savaged with an inspirational toilet roll. A 'Thought for Today' on every leaf. That driver was having a few thoughts for today of his own, wasn't he? I had to buy two dozen to cool him down. What am I going to do with two dozen inspirational toilet rolls?

[**Granville** *smiles*]

Arkwright: And I don't want earthy s-suggestions from you, thank you Cinderella. Right, you can take that lot down to the cellar, or you'll never go to the ball.

Granville: You'll have to open the trap. I've got me hands full.

Arkwright: It's me who's got me hands full, coping with a speed-crazed Hungarian like you.

Granville: There's no variety in my life.

[**Arkwright** *opens the trap-door*]

Arkwright: You're going down the cellar, aren't you? How much variety do you need in one day?

Granville: I don't know why you get rid of your van.

Arkwright: You don't know why I got rid of the van.

Granville: [*from inside the cellar*] Because you couldn't sleep every time they put petrol up.

Arkwright: And while you're down there, clear that cellar out. And if you do find an old lamp, for God's sake don't rub it.

Granville: [*To himself*] If I've got to keep riding that shop bike, I'm going to get it done up a bit. A few accessories.

[*A customer enters the shop.* **Arkwright** *comes round to greet her, rubbing his hands together. His smile slips a bit when he sees that it is* **Mavis** *again. She is swaying slightly*]

Arkwright: Oh, it's you again, Mavis.

[*She holds out a packet of detergent*]

Mavis: On second thoughts, Mr Arkwright, I think I'll take the other brand.

[*He takes it from her with a sigh*]

Arkwright: You're quite sh-sure about this?

Mavis: Yes, I've made me mind up.

Arkwright: You sound very sure of yourself. Have you been having a nip at the sherry again?

[**Mavis** *grins wickedly*]

Mavis: It changes me whole personality. Shopping becomes a completely new experience.

Arkwright: I'll fetch a packet from the warehouse. While I'm gone, tr-try and keep your eyes off this new line in inspirational toilet rolls, which are already spoken for. You know I'd let you have some if it was up to me.

Mavis: New line, is it?

Arkwright: It's no good. Don't tempt yourself.

[*He goes through to the warehouse.* **Mavis** *prods a toilet roll experimentally*]

Granville: [*From the cellar*] Hey up!

[**Mavis** *jumps guiltily and looks everywhere for the source of the voice*]

Granville: I'm talking to you. Can you hear me?

[**Mavis** *twists her head about, trying to locate the sound*]

Granville: Is there anybody there? [*There is a pause*] Where's he gone?

Mavis: He's in the warehouse.

Granville: Who's that?

Mavis: They call me Mavis.

Granville: Hello, Mavis.

[**Mavis** *looks round nervously, her eyes wide*]

Mavis: Hello.

[**Arkwright** *returns from the warehouse carrying another packet*]

Arkwright: Here we are then. And if you d-don't like this one, there's only Brand X.

[**Mavis** *crosses to the counter, and clutches his arm*]

Mavis: Mr Arkwright, I heard a little voice.

Arkwright: Oh heck! [*He slams the packet on the counter*] And I suppose it's been telling you to ch-change back to the other detergent?

Mavis: No.

Arkwright: No?

Mavis: No.

Arkwright: Oh.

Mavis: It said – 'Hallo, Mavis'.

[**Arkwright** *puts two and two together*]

Arkwright: Oh, did it! [*He sneaks a glance down the cellar and then smiles wickedly. He turns to* **Mavis** *reassuringly*] 'Hallo Mavis' it said, did it? Well, that sounds friendly enough. It doesn't appear to everybody. I think you're in luck.

Mavis: Who could it be, Mr Arkwright?

Arkwright: We've made ex-er-haustive enquiries and we've reached the conclusion that it's the spirit of some V-Victorian shopkeeper who likes to keep his finger on the pulse of the trade.

Mavis: [*Alarmed*] His finger?

Arkwright: Only m-metaphorically – nothing you need tell your husband about. He's got a wonderful eye for a superior product. If you were f-fortunate enough to hear him recommend today's best buys, then I wouldn't hesitate. [*He moves her away from the counter*] Tell you what, Mavis, the place to stand for the best reception is about here. Cl-close your eyes and concentrate. Speak, O Experienced One.

[**Granville** *appears up the steps*]

Granville: You what?

[**Arkwright** *pushes him down again with his foot*]

Arkwright: What, in your opinion, is today's best buy?

[*He waves a packet of fig biscuits at* **Granville**]

Granville: Fig biscuits?

Arkwright: Pardon, oh Learned One?

Granville: [*With more conviction*] Fig biscuits.

Arkwright: What did he say, Mavis?

Mavis: [*Turning*] It sounded like fig biscuits.

Arkwright: I thought that as well. He gives all me bargains away. Wait a minute – he's coming through with something else. Turn the other way, Mavis.

[*He shows* **Granville** *a toilet roll*]

Granville: Inspirational toilet rolls.

Arkwright: Again, Sir Jasper.

Granville: Inspirational toilet rolls.

Arkwright: That's it. And how many should the lady take to ensure good luck?

Granville: [*Tentatively*] Two?

[**Arkwright** *throws the toilet roll at* **Granville**]

Granville: Oh hell . . .

Arkwright: [*Threateningly*] How many?

Granville: . . . elve . . . Tw . . . twelve. Twelve.

Arkwright: Twelve, Oh I see. Thank you. Over and out.

[*He closes the trap.* **Mavis** *moves to the counter*]

Arkwright: Aren't you lucky, Mavis? You've been given both bargains. Twelve inspirational toilet rolls and one packet of fig biscuits. There we are, Mavis. Four pounds exactly. [*He crosses to the door and opens it.* **Mavis** *crosses and exits*] Mind how you go. Oh no, you won't need to now, will you? You can go as often as you like. And with them fig biscuits I think you'll need that lot.

11   Inside the shop

Granville: You shouldn't pull her leg like that.

Arkwright: Listen, you've no time for scr-scruples where you've over-bought on inspirational toilet rolls. [*He rearranges the remaining ones*] That's twelve down, twelve to go.

Granville: Can I have a bun?

Arkwright: Of course you can have a bun. There's more than enough. Do I ever deprive you of anything?

Granville: [*Offering a tentative suggestion*] A satisfactory love-life?

Arkwright: Eat your bun. [**Granville** *takes a bit.* **Arkwright** *watches*] All right, is it?

Granville: Delicious. I didn't think you'd let me have one.

Arkwright: Oh Granville, you w-wound me at times.

Granville: Oh do I? When?

Arkwright: Well, that time I sat on your bicycle clips springs to mind. Cream nice and fresh, is it?

Granville: Lovely.

Arkwright: I've never been mean with you. Have I?

Granville: Not just with me. With everybody.

Arkwright: Its just a façade. And do remember I raised you from this high. [*He makes a suitable sign with his hand*] Admittedly not very far.

Granville: I'm too small for elegant women, aren't I?

Arkwright: Look on the bright side. You're the perfect size for a shop bike.

[**Granville** *groans and looks round for somewhere to wipe his fingers.* **Arkwright** *reaches for a toilet roll, opens it and* *passes one to the surprised* **Granville**]

Arkwright: Here, you can use a bit of this.

Granville: Ta! You're being very agreeable today.

Arkwright: A little thoughtfulness never goes amiss.

Granville: Is that what it says there?

Arkwright: No. I said that. This says,
'If you've a dirty job to do get a grip on it,
Get stuck in and see it through, get a grip on it.
Life's a big stick that will not bend
And if a man you thought a friend
Has handed you the mucky end
  get a grip on it.
Now wash your hands.' That'll be 50p.

Granville: 50p? For one bun?

Arkwright: And the rest of the roll. You can put some cheese on it.

[**Granville** *sighs and reaches for his wallet*]

Arkwright: Don't moan. I've knocked you 5p off.

[*He takes* **Granville's** *pound and walks round the counter, examining the note as he goes. He holds it up to the light*]

Arkwright: You wouldn't get a sound economic training like this anywhere else, you kno-o-o-oh!

[*He disappears down the cellar.* **Granville** *suppresses an urge to titter, but winces a bit at the sounds of* **Arkwright's** *descent*]

Granville: Shall I close the door? Or do you like the draught?

12   The street outside the shop

Nurse Gladys *stops her car and hurries round to help* **Arkwright,** *who has a stick, and his foot in plaster.*

Nurse: Give me your hand. [*She slaps his wrist*] Not there. You're worse on one leg than you are on two.

Arkwright: You've got to make allowances for sh-shock.

Nurse: When I'm with you I know all about shock. You've given me half a dozen driving you home from the surgery.

[**Arkwright** *grins happily*]

Arkwright: I was just holding your knee for luck.

Nurse: Well your luck ran out, didn't it.

Arkwright: It did. I never th-thought you'd hit a cripple. Especially there. At a busy junction.

Nurse: Put your arm round me neck. [*She plans to help him out of the car, but he pulls her in*] Give over, you great fool!

[*In her struggles she pips the hooter.* **Granville** *comes from the shop and gapes at the struggle in the car*]

Nurse: What are you doing?

Arkwright: Keep quiet. I'll think of something.

Granville: Is he having a fit?

Arkwright: Well I'm game if she is.

Nurse: Help me get him on his feet.

[*They get* **Arkwright** *on the pavement and hand him his stick*]

Nurse: Ooh, it's like fighting off a gang a pickpockets.

[*They watch* **Arkwright** *hobble smartly into the shop*]

Granville: How's his leg?

Nurse: He'll be all right. It's his hands that ought to be in plaster.

Granville: Look at him. He can't wait to get inside and make sure I've not ruined his business while he's been away.

Nurse: He thought about you.

Granville: Did he?

Nurse: While he was still drowsy from the anaesthetic.

Granville: No. Go on! Did he?

Nurse: Ring our Granville, he said. See if he's sold them other twelve toilet rolls.

[**Granville** *groans*]

13 Outside the shop

It is dark, and **Arkwright** *is closing up the shop, hobbling a bit as he takes his pavement items in*]

Arkwright: [*To himself*] Ah well, it's been a funny day. I'll get closed up and give Nurse Gladys Emmanuel a ring. I'm a bona fide patient now. She ought to come over and have a look at things. [*Pause*] Even if it's only me foot. [*Pause*] I wonder what a State Registered Nurse would do for twelve inspirational toilet rolls. [*Pause*] I hope our Granville's not going to be out too late. Up to his Hungarian tricks. [*Looking up*] Oh Lord, if you're listening, keep him away from expensive women. Especially that lot down where he keeps losing his bicycle clips. And P.S. Lord, remind our Granville in future to keep his tr-trap shut.

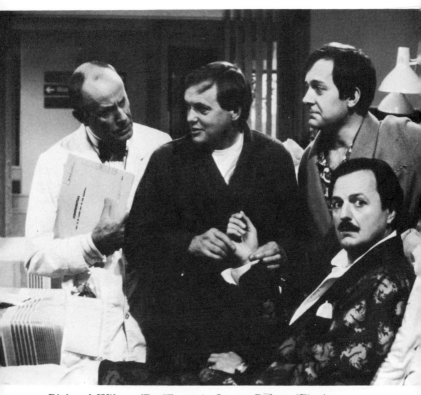

Richard Wilson (Dr Thorpe), James Bolam (Figgis),
Christopher Strauli (Norman) and Peter Bowles (Glover) in
the Yorkshire Television series Only When I Laugh
(Yorkshire Television copyright)

Only When I Laugh:
A Day in the Life Of
Eric Chappell

First shown on Yorkshire Television on 2 September 1981

Characters

Figgis
Glover } patients in the hospital
Norman
Thorpe, a doctor
Gupte, a male nurse
Gary, a television producer
Phil, a television director
Camera crew

Only When I Laugh: A Day in the Life Of

---

1   A ward in a hospital

Figgis *and* **Norman** *are in their beds;* **Gupte** *is tidying the ward.*

   We catch a glimpse of a television camera crew in the corridor.

   Gupte *begins fussing around* **Figgis'** *locker.*

Figgis: [*Disgusted*] Have you noticed something? Have you noticed how tidy we've become since the television cameras arrived?

Gupte: What do you expect, Figgis? We're going to be on television. We don't want everything in a muddle.

Figgis: Why not? Why don't we have the usual grotty mess with a few dead bodies lying around? This isn't going to capture the reality of the situation, everyone going around with toothpaste smiles and being unnaturally nice to each other.

Gupte: That's nonsense, Figgis. We are all being perfectly natural.

Figgis: If you're being perfectly natural – where are your glasses?

Gupte: [*Coyly*] Well, I didn't want to wear them today. I was afraid the lights might reflect on the lens. Besides . . . I think I look better without them.

Figgis: I know, but you can't see as well, can you? You keep bumping into things. I just hope you're not called upon to give an injection, that's all.

[**Gupte** *goes out*]

Figgis: Did you hear that? He thinks he looks better without them. It's going to be a complete waste of time – they're going to give a totally false impression.

Norman: [*Earnestly*] That's where you're wrong, Figgis. They always say no matter how you try and cover things up the camera never lies.

Figgis: No, but it can stretch it a bit – especially round here. Look at Thorpe – he's being all sweetness and light. Why can't he act naturally and be the normal, 'orrible person we've all come to know and hate? And why does he have to hog the camera so much?

Norman: Well, it is supposed to be a day in his life, Figgis.

Figgis: Yes, and whose idea was that? It's always the doctors – never the patients. Who's taking the risks around here? We are. And we never get a look in. All you get is a trembling hand coming out of the blankets and a quavering voice saying 'God bless you, doctor.' It's always been the same, ever since Doctor Kildare. Faceless patients, and Richard Chamberlain having it away at the country club.

[**Glover** *enters*]

Glover: [*Excitedly*] They're coming this way! They're coming this way!

Figgis: Well, you needn't worry, Archie, they won't come in here.

Glover: Nevertheless, I think I'll just slip a comb through my hair. You never know.

Figgis: Just listen to him. He's been chasing around after them all morning. A real camera freak, aren't you, Archie?

Glover: Certainly not, Figgis. I'm just curious to see what's going on, that's all.

Norman: What's Thorpe doing now, Archie?

Glover: They're shooting him coming down the corridor.

Figgis: Shooting him? That's the best idea they've had all day.

Glover: That's a technical term, Figgis. It means they're filming him coming down the corridor.

Norman: But he's been doing that for the last hour.

Glover: They don't like his walk.

Figgis: Well, neither do I but I don't see why we should have it on film.

Glover: He's making a real mess of it. All he had to do this morning was get out of his car – pick up his briefcase and walk into the hospital. It took him two hours. First of all he got his foot caught in the safety belt and fell out of the car – then he forgot his briefcase – and when he finally entered the hospital he walked straight into a glass door. It was an absolute shambles. Gary and Phil didn't like it at all.

Figgis: You mean those two blokes in the pink shirts?

Glover: [*Loftily*] The producer and the director, Figgis.

Figgis: Yeh, they look as if they'd be more at home with *Jackanory*. The first sight of a real disease and they'd be straight out of those doors. If they want real drama they should come in here. They don't want a day in the life of Gordon Thorpe – they want a day in the death of Royston Figgis.

Glover: Just as I thought. You want to get in front of those cameras, don't you, Figgis?

Figgis: I wouldn't mind. At least I could speak up for the patients – tell the truth about this hospital.

Norman: I was on television once.

Figgis: Were you, Norman? What were you doing?

Norman: I was holding a tin of beans.

Figgis: You mean it was a commercial?

Norman: No, closed circuit at Tesco's. I looked quite good. In fact I think I'd make a good television performer.

Figgis: Doing what?

Norman: Well, presenting *Blue Peter* or *Magpie* – sitting around in jeans and a jersey – talking to the children and showing them how to make things out of egg packets. I'd be good at that.

Glover: Yes, I always think I'd go down well on the box. You see, what television needs today is a new face.

Figgis: There's nothing new about your face, Archie.

Glover: There would be on television. What we need is a new approach. A return to style and glamour and the days of Macdonald Hobley. [*Pause*] I think I'd better go and freshen myself up.

Figgis: Give over. You're only trying to get in front of those cameras again. You'll be there grinning away with the rest of them.

Glover: I've no intention of doing anything so vulgar, Figgis. No, if they want me they'll have to ask for me.

2   The corridor outside the ward

The camera crew has set the camera up and is waiting to start filming. **Thorpe** *is preparing to walk into shot. He is being supervised by* **Gary** *and* **Phil** *– two earnest young men in jeans.*

Gary: Now do you think you could try that walk down the corridor again, Mr Thorpe? But this time try and forget the camera. It's just an ordinary morning – keep the walk perfectly natural.

Thorpe: Perfectly natural. Right, Gary.

Phil: [*To one of the crew*] Put a slate up. OK. Action.

Thorpe: From here?

Phil: [*He sighs*] Yes, Mr Thorpe.

Thorpe: Ready?

Phil: [*Wearily*] Yes.

Thorpe: I'm coming . . . now.

[*He walks down the corridor in a brisk exaggerated manner with many embellishments*]

Phil: [*To the crew*] Cut! [*Quietly, to* **Gary**] He's over the top again, Gary.

Gary: Yes. I'm afraid it's Mickey Mouse time, Phil. [*Louder*] Mr Thorpe, do you always walk like that?

Thorpe: Well, yes, I think so.

Phil: Well, do you think you could do it a little slower with less flourish this time?

Thorpe: Less flourish. Certainly.

Phil: Right. Action.

[**Thorpe** *begins his walk.* **Glover** *walks into shot*]

Glover: Good morning, Mr Thorpe.

Thorpe: [*Through clenched teeth, trying not to let* **Glover** *intimidate him*] Keep walking, Glover.

Glover: I beg your pardon?

Thorpe: Go away.

Glover: Is there something wrong with your teeth, doctor?

Thorpe: [*Giving in*] I'm being filmed, Glover.

Glover: Oh! [*He feigns surprise and beams at the camera*] I didn't realize there were cameras. I seem to have blown the whole thing. I do apologize. Excuse me.

[*He exits still beaming at the camera*]

Phil: Cut! Don't worry, Mr Thorpe. I think we've got enough. Now if we could pick you up walking straight into the ward.

Thorpe: [*Nervously*] In here?

Phil: If you would, please.

Thorpe: Do I have to?

Gary: We are in a hurry, Mr Thorpe.

Figgis: [*Sighing*] Very well.

Phil: Right. Action.

[**Thorpe** *approaches the door with a casual air. He pushes it with his fingers, just as* **Figgis** *pushes it from the other side. There is a collision and* **Thorpe** *is thrown backwards*]

Thorpe: [*Angrily*] Figgis, you fool – can't you see I'm being filmed?

Figgis: Are you? Where? Oh, I see. [*He nods at the camera*] Hallo. I didn't realize, but since I'm here perhaps you'd like me to say a few words.

Thorpe: Certainly not.

Figgis: I could express the patients' point of view. I do have a few comments to make that may be of interest to the viewer.

Thorpe: Gupte! Get Figgis back in bed at once.

Gupte: Certainly, Mr Thorpe.

[*He takes* **Figgis'** *arm and beams at the camera*]

Thorpe: [*Staring incredulously at* **Gupte**] Gupte, what's happened to your glasses?

Gupte: [*Smirking*] I took them off. I thought I looked better without them.

Thorpe: [*Sighing*] Just take Figgis back to his bed, will you?

Figgis: All right – if you want a bland, boring film with no human interest, that's your affair.

Gupte: Come, Figgis.

[*They return to the ward with* **Gupte** *beaming at the camera and* **Figgis** *giving it a farewell wave*]

Thorpe: Sorry about that, Gary.

Gary: Never mind, Mr Thorpe – there's always one.

Phil: [*Under his breath*] There's more than one.

3   The ward

Thorpe, Gary *and* **Phil** *enter the ward.* **Norman** *and* **Figgis** *are in bed.*

Gary: Now, Mr Thorpe, we want you to go across to a patient and talk to him – so that we can observe your understanding and compassion.

Thorpe: [*Grumpily*] Yes, well let's get it over with while I've still got some left.

Phil: Right. Just give us a dummy run, Mr Thorpe.

[**Thorpe** *looks along the beds.* **Figgis** *smiles invitingly. He ignores him and turns to* **Norman**]

Thorpe: Well, Norman, old chap – how are you feeling today?

Gary: Could you hold his hand, Mr Thorpe?

Thorpe: [*Nervously*] What?

Gary: Just to show the compassion.

Thorpe: Yes, I see. Norman, could I hold your hand?

Norman: Certainly, Mr Thorpe.

[*They hold hands awkwardly*]

Gary: And look into his eyes when you're talking to him. We want to feel the warmth. The feeling of a kindly father figure. [*To* **Phil**] I think we've got something here, Phil. He's got a wonderful face.

Phil: [*Softly*] Business before pleasure, Gary.

Thorpe: How are you feeling today, old chap?

Norman: [*Enunciating ridiculously clearly*] Very much better, thank you, doctor – and may I say it's due to your skill and care that I find myself in this happy position after months of pain.

Thorpe: Splendid. You'll soon be on your feet again – punting the leather – playing football with the best of them.

Norman: Yes, I'm looking forward to that, doctor. I'm looking forward to playing football with the best of them.

Thorpe: Splendid.

Gary: I think that's enough, Mr Thorpe. We'll just set the lights – then we'll do it for real. Should we have a coffee?

Thorpe: Certainly, Gary.

[*They exit*]

Norman: [*Excitedly*] I'm going to be on television, Figgis! I'm going to be on television!

Figgis: [*Enviously*] Yes, I suppose you are. [*Slyly*] Well, I just hope you can pull it off, that's all. As long as you don't have any trouble with the old nerves you should be all right.

Norman: I don't have any trouble with my nerves, Figgis.

Figgis: Come on. When you're under pressure you start getting that twitch – that little muscle in your cheek starts to work. All that's going to show on television you know. They're going to see every crafty movement of your eyes. Every uncertainty. The involuntary lick of your dry lips – the beads of sweat on your brow. Your total falseness revealed to millions.

Norman: What falseness? What do you mean, Figgis?

Figgis: The camera may never lie but you certainly do. You've never played football in your life.

Norman: Well, no . . . but I've played table tennis.

Figgis: That's not the same thing at all. You were sitting there passing yourself off as a second Kevin Keegan.

[*One of the crew approaches and fixes a microphone to* **Norman**]

Norman: [*Nervously*] What's that for?

Phil: It's a mike.

Figgis: You see – now you're wired for every sound – I just hope your stomach doesn't start rumbling.

Norman: I'm afraid I'll have to take it off – I've got to go somewhere.

Figgis: Well, they certainly don't want to hear you in there.

[**Norman** *rips off the microphone and dashes off*]

Figgis: Nerves – you see. Always gets the bladder first.

4   The ward

It is half an hour later, and all the lights have been assembled for the filming. **Norman** *clears his throat nervously.*

Phil: Ready, everyone? Right. Action.

Thorpe: How are you feeling today, old chap?

Norman: Very much better, thank you, doctor. [*He stops and turns to* **Gary**] Excuse me. Should we hold hands now or later?

Phil: [*To the crew*] Cut.

Gary: Hold hands whenever you feel like it, Norman.

Figgis: Chase me.

Thorpe: [*peevishly*] Should we start again?

Norman: Sorry.

Phil: Action.

Thorpe: How are you feeling today, old chap?

Norman: Very much better, thank you, doctor. And may I say it's due to your kill and scare that I find myself –

Thorpe: Wait a minute. He said kill and scare.

Gary: He's right, Phil. He said kill and scare.

Figgis: Of course he did. It's what they call a Freudian slip.

Thorpe: It was not a Freudian slip, Figgis. He simply got it the wrong way round.

Figgis: Yeah – it should have been scare and kill.

Gary: Right. Let's try again.

Norman: Sorry.

Phil: Action.

Thorpe: [*with less warmth*] Well, how are you feeling today, old chap?

Norman: Very much better, doctor. And may I say it's due to your skill and care that I find myself in the ... in the happy position in which I now find myself in the present time ... in.

Thorpe: [*Horrified*] My God! The boy's waffling. We can't go on like this.

Norman: Sorry everyone.

Phil: Now don't worry, Norman. Let's try again. Action.

Thorpe: [*Through gritted teeth*] Well, and how are you feeling today, old chap?

Norman: [*Carefully*] Very much better, thank you, doctor. And may I say that it's due to your skill and care that I find myself in this happy position after pain of months

Thorpe: [*He erupts*] He said pain of months! We can't go on like this. The whole thing's ridiculous.

Gary: But we must show your understanding and compassion, Mr Thorpe.

Thorpe: Then get someone else. The boy's a fool.

[**Glover** *enters*]

Glover: [*Smoothly*] Having trouble?

[*They turn and look at* **Glover***. He is looking particularly impressive. He is wearing a resplendent dressing gown and is leaning dramatically on a walking stick. There is a slim book of verse under his arm.* **Gary** *and* **Phil** *look at him approvingly.*]

Glover: Oh, you're filming again. I didn't realize. I've been out on the terrace reading a little Wordsworth. We both have the same feeling for nature. I find it a great solace ... watching the leaves fall and knowing that after Autumn there's always another Spring.

[*He sighs and smiles bravely*]

Phil: What do you think, Gary?

Gary: Wonderful stuff, Phil.

[*The whole crew move towards* **Glover's** *bed*]

Gary: Could you come over here, Mr Thorpe?

Norman: [*Unhappily*] Hey! What about me?

Figgis: Never mind, Norman. That's show business.

5   The ward

It is a few minutes later. The crew are setting up the lights again.
Figgis *and* **Norman** *are watching enviously from their beds.*
Glover *is giving himself a final preening at the table.* **Phil**
enters.

Phil: Will you be ready soon, Mr Glover?

Glover: Just teasing out a few curls, Phil. It's not every day
one appears on television. Do you think this dressing
gown'll suit – will you be able to pick out the colours?

Phil: Yes – that'll be fine.

Glover: And what about make-up?

Phil: That won't be necessary.

Glover: Oh.

Figgis: Never mind, Archie – you've still got time to take it
off.

Glover: I'm not wearing it, Figgis. Actually, it's times like
this when I thank God for a good skin. Now I want you to
get my best side, Phil – so what position do you think I
should take up?

Norman: Face downwards.

Glover: [*Sharply*] Don't be petty, Norman. You've had your chance – now it's mine.

Phil: [*Uneasily*] I would like to point out, Mr Glover – it is supposed to be a film about the doctor.

Glover: Yes, but let's be frank, even his best friends wouldn't call him handsome. He's too colourless. I think he'll come over rather beige. It'll be about as exciting as watching a plank warp. Still, you know your business best. Just tell me where the cameras are.

Phil: Don't worry, Mr Glover. We'll look after everything. [*He begins to leave*]

Glover: Yes, well, don't let's get too disciplined. I can be rather inventive, so if I do anything unexpected, keep the cameras rolling.

Phil: [*More uneasily*] Yes, well, just let us know when you're ready, Mr Glover . . . and try to keep it natural.

[*He goes out*]

Norman: [*Bitterly*] Natural! He's about as natural as a plastic daffodil.

Glover: [*Smugly*] Eat your heart out, Norman Binns – you're only jealous.

Figgis: He's right, Norman. We shouldn't be envious.

Glover: [*Surprised*] That's decent of you, Figgis. I rather thought you wanted to be on.

Figgis: I wouldn't have minded but that's not the point. The big thing is that one of the patients is going to get a look in for a change. That's important – so watch Thorpe. He'll try and mask you, Archie.

Glover: What do you mean?

Figgis: I mean he'll stand in front so no one can see you.

Glover: Will he indeed?

Norman: Or he'll upstage you.

Glover: Upstage me? What's that exactly, Norman?

Norman: He'll keep turning you towards him so that you've got your back to the camera.

Figgis: You see, we want you to look good, Archie. Patients are always portrayed as empty husks just lying around whilst the medical staff get all the glamour. This is your chance to redress the balance. This could lead to something, Archie. You could be reading the news this time next year. You could be another Angela Rippon. Guest appearances on *Call my Bluff* or, dare we say it, *Blankety-Blank*. But it won't happen if all we see is the back of your head.

Glover: [*Grimly*] Don't worry, Figgis – they won't be seeing the back of my head, I can assure you.

Figgis: Good for you, Archie. And don't forget, plenty of business with the old stick – and the old book of verse – and plenty of those perceptive insights.

Glover: You're right Figgis. I think the viewer'll be particularly interested in my philosophy of life. [*He stands up*] You can tell them I'm ready.

[**Figgis** *exits*]

6   The corridor

Thorpe *is standing away from the activity taking deep breaths by the window.* **Figgis** *enters.*

Thorpe: Isn't he ready yet, Figgis?

Figgis: Just about, Doctor.

Thorpe: Then let's get on with it.

Figgis: I'd just like to say – I'm sorry the way things are going.

Thorpe: What do you mean – the way things are going?

Figgis: Well, after all, it is supposed to be about a day in your life. There's not going to be much chance of that with old Greta Garbo in there. The trouble is everyone's trying to get in on the act.

Thorpe: Yes, including you, Figgis.

Figgis: Well, at least I'm not taller than you. He's six-foot-two, Doctor. He's going to make you look like a dwarf – you'll be trotting beside him like Quasimodo. You'll be lucky to get your head in.

Thorpe: You're forgetting something, Figgis – the camera will be trained on me.

Figgis: I'm not so sure. He's looking good, doctor. He's been slapping rouge on ever since this thing started – and I'm sure he's borrowed some eye shadow from Sister. Just don't let him upstage you, that's all.

Thorpe: How can he upstage me, Figgis?

Figgis: By turning you away from the camera so that all we see is that bald spot on the back of your head. It's an old trick. He'll be smiling into the camera and you'll be just a white coat flapping around . . .

Thorpe: We'll see about that, Figgis.

[**Gupte** *enters. He has just shaved off his moustache*]

Gupte: They are ready for you now, Mr Thorpe.

[**Thorpe** *stares at him in astonishment*]

Thorpe: Gupte – what's happened to your moustache?

Gupte: I have shaved it off. I thought I'd look better without it. I think I look more interesting – don't you agree?

Thorpe: No, I don't. It's my life they're doing, not yours. You won't be going in front of the cameras – all they see is possibly your hand as you pass me the case notes. So stop this charade and grow it again at once!

[**Thorpe** *storms away towards the ward*]

7   The ward

The television crew have assembled. **Glover** *and* **Thorpe** *are standing in the centre of the ward.*

Phil: Now all we want you to do is to walk down the centre of the ward, Mr Thorpe, with Mr Glover – seeing him to his bed and passing the time of day. Right? Action.

Glover: Er . . . could someone just dab my brow? I think I'm beginning to glisten a little.

Gupte: Certainly, Mr Glover.

[**Gupte** *dabs* **Glover's** *forehead and beams at the camera*]

Phil: Right. Action.

Gary: [*Raising his hand to signal to the crew that he is not ready for them to start*] I was just wondering – just a suggestion. Do you think you could put a hand on his shoulder, Mr Thorpe?

Thorpe: Certainly not. He's too tall. If you want me to do that he'll have to crouch.

Glover: I'm not going to crouch. I'd look ridiculous.

Gary: [*Soothingly*] It was just a thought. Carry on.

Phil: Right. Action.

[**Thorpe** *and* **Glover** *walk down the ward, gently jostling for position in front of camera*]

Thorpe: [*Briskly*] Ah, Glover. I've seen the results of your tests – everything's fine. You should be out of here in no time at all.

[*He tries to sweep* **Glover** *towards the bed.* **Glover** *refuses to be hurried. He turns* **Thorpe** *slowly round so that he has his back to camera*]

Glover: Wait a minute, doctor. I wouldn't be leaning so heavily on this stick if everything was fine. You can tell me the truth – I can take it. After all, what is life but a game played by fools . . . ?

[*They start to circle around each other as they attempt to get into shot*]

Thorpe: [*Desperately*] Glover, I can assure you there's nothing wrong with you.

Glover: I'm just happy that I've led a full life. I've crammed more into my few years than most people could have done in a lifetime. 'I warmed both hands before the fire of life; it sinks and I am ready to depart.'

Thorpe: [*Angrily*] Then why don't you, Glover? [*Turning to* **Gary**] Is he going to go on like this all the time? It's supposed to be a day in my life – not his.

Glover: I was trying to add a little colour. *I* can't help it if you look bad, Thorpe.

Thorpe: [*Aroused*] I don't look bad – I don't look anything – I can't get a look in – not with you gabbling.

Glover: I'm not gabbling. And whilst we're on the subject, stop trying to hog the camera – I mean your face isn't exactly going to launch a thousand ships, is it?

Thorpe: That's it, Gary. I refuse to go on.

Gary: I'm sorry, Mr Glover.

Glover: What?

Gary: I'm afraid we'll have to find someone else.

Glover: Oh, I see – it's amateur night, is it?

[*He stalks off*]

Gary: Sorry, Phil.

Phil: [*Despairingly*] Can't we find someone who'll seem more like an ordinary patient?

[*They turn and look at* **Figgis.** *He smiles back at them innocently*]

Thorpe: [*With a groan*] Oh, no, not Figgis!

8   The ward

It is half an hour later. Lights have been assembled around **Figgis'** *bed.* **Norman** *and* **Glover** *have been moved to one side and are watching enviously.*

Glover: Just look at him, Norman. The lengths some people will go to get their faces on television. How could they chose anyone so grotesque – and that hideous dressing gown.

Norman: I never thought he'd be like that, Archie. The way he's creeping around Thorpe. I thought at least he'd stand up for the patients.

Figgis: [*Earnestly*] Now, Mr Thorpe, I want to get this right. Just tell me what you want me to say and I'll say it. After all, it's your show – we're just your acolytes, really. What was it again?

Thorpe: All you have to say is 'I'm feeling a little better today thank you, Mr Thorpe.'

Figgis: Now let me get that right. 'I'm feeling a little better today, thank you.' Yes, I think I've got that. You see, I want to memorize it. I don't want to have to extemporize. It's important we both know what we're doing. Would you like to hold my hand, doctor?

Thorpe:　No, I don't think that'll be necessary, Figgis.

Figgis:　Please yourself, Doctor. Am I all wired up properly, Gary?

Gary:　Yes, Mr Figgis. Now this is going to be very brief because we're running out of time.

Figgis:　Yes, I quite understand, I'll just try and follow Mr Thorpe's lead. I won't move too much because I don't want to mask him from the camera or anything. I'll just sit back here – or perhaps you'd like me lying down with my hands showing?

Phil:　No, sitting up will be fine, Mr Figgis.

Figgis:　Sitting up like this? Well, if that's all right with you, Mr Thorpe.

Phil:　Good. Are you ready to go, Mr Thorpe?

Thorpe:　Yes, I'm ready.

Figgis:　Right. And don't hurry anything, Mr Thorpe, because I'll just be sitting here watching you. Good luck, everyone.

Phil:　Right. Action.

Thorpe:　Well, Figgis, and how are you today?

[**Figgis** *straightens up. A gleam comes into his eye as the trap closes*]

Figgis:　I'm glad you asked me that, doctor. Because for some time I've been having these terrible pains in the stomach and whenever I complain about them I'm told not to worry. I'm not a fool, doctor – if there's nothing to worry about, why all the X-Rays? I'm not right down here [*Pointing beneath blankets*], and you know it. The job's been botched and I want to know what you're going to do about it.

Thorpe: [*Panicking*] Don't be ridiculous, Figgis. All you have is a mild post-operative infection.

Figgis: Yes, and why? Because the hygiene in this hospital leaves a great deal to be desired. We've got the highest fatality rate in the country. Streptococci is rampant in the canteen – it's the only thing that gives the food any taste.

Thorpe: There's nothing wrong with the food, Figgis.

Figgis: There's nothing right with it. It's all out of packets. Where's the goodness in that? They should throw the food away and boil the packets – at least we'd get more vitamins.

[*He gets out of bed and throws the blankets back so that he can make his points more eloquently. The camera keeps turning*]

Thorpe: Figgis, get back into bed at once.

Figgis: No, it's time someone stood up for the patients. Everybody ignores us. It's time we were heard. We won't be kept in ignorance any longer. And that's my main complaint. No one tells you a bloody thing.

Thorpe: There's nothing to tell, Figgis. You're making a perfect recovery.

Figgis: [*Grimly*] I'm making a perfect recovery, am I? Is that what you think? Then cop a load of this.

[**Figgis** *opens his dressing gown to the camera. There is a groan and the* **Cameraman** *slumps forward*]

Gary: [*Excitedly*] Keep it rolling – this is exciting television!

Thorpe: Stop the camera!

[*He tries to cover* **Figgis** *with a blanket*]

Figgis: [*Struggling*] That's right – sweep the truth under the carpet. Let's have a bland film – all sweetness and light. Never mind what we have to put up with in this place.

Thorpe: [*Desperately*] Gupte! Do something.

[**Gupte** *dashes forward*]

Gupte: Leave this to me, Mr Thorpe.

[**Thorpe** *stares at him in astonishment. Not only has* **Gupte** *shed his glasses and moustache – he has now restyled his hair*]

Thorpe: Gupte! What have you done to your hair?

Gupte: [*Beams*] I thought it would look better for the camera.

Thorpe: [*He groans*] Oh no!

Figgis: Let go. Let me speak.

Gupte: Please be calm, Mr Figgis. [*Ogling camera*] You can trust Gupte. Isn't he always here when you need him – long after the doctors are home in bed? Always with a cheery smile and a cup of tea – pushing back the hours of darkness.

Norman: [*Moving determinedly into shot*] Gupte's right, Roy. You shouldn't complain – it's a wonderful hospital. [*He smiles at the camera*] They work miracles here everyday. I for one can't speak too highly of them.

Glover: [*Pushing forward*] He's right, Roy. Don't whine – be a man. Take life as it comes. Face it squarely in the eye. Live each day as though it were your last.

Thorpe: [*Struggling to be seen*] Do you mind? This is my show.

Figgis: Enough of these platitudes, Archie. [*Struggling* *forward*] Let's tell them the truth for a change. Let's show the public what it's really like.

Thorpe: But it's supposed to be about *me*. It's a day in *my* life – not yours, Figgis!

[*They continue to struggle and shout. The camera sways alarmingly, and the scene turns into pandemonium*]

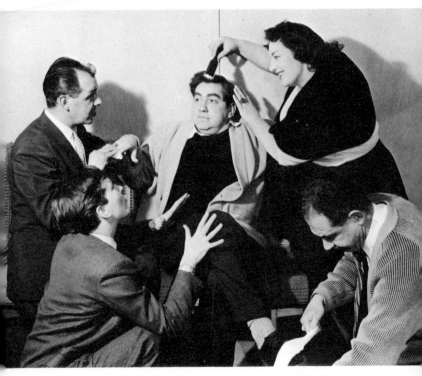

Tony Hancock being 'groomed for the part' by Kenneth Williams, Bill Kerr, Hattie Jacques and Sid James, the cast of Hancock's Half Hour *on radio. (BBC copyright)*

Hancock's Half Hour:
The Bowmans
Ray Galton and Alan Simpson

Characters

Tony, who plays Joshua Merryweather in 'The Bowmans'
A radio producer
A radio announcer

Other characters in 'The Bowmans'

Dan Bowman (played by **Windthrift Osmington**)
Mrs Bowman (played by **Celia Beaumont**)
George
Dog (played by an **actor**)
Fred
Diane
Doctor

Julian Court, an actor
Auditioning Shakespearean actor
A voice
Advertisement director
Advertisement announcer
Girl in advert *(non-speaking)*
Postman
Porter
Reporter
Head official

Actor
Pageboys
BBC officials

Hancock's Half Hour: The Bowmans

---

1   Inside a radio studio

We see a sign reading 'On the Air'; the production staff are sitting in the control box, behind a plate-glass window. We hear linking music, and the **producer** *signals the cast to begin the next scene. The cast members of the programme are grouped around a microphone in the studio, and they all have scripts in their hands. At the signal from the* **producer***, the* **announcer** *steps forward and speaks through the microphone.*

Announcer: Meanwhile, back at Brook Farm, Dan Bowman has his troubles too.

Dan Bowman: Well, those blasted crows have certainly taken all the seed out of this field, George.

George: Ah, you're right there, gaffer. If we don't get a decent crop out of this field, we won't have any winter feeding for the cows.

Dan Bowman: That's true. Oh this farming life! If it's not one thing, it's another.

George: Ah, yes.

Dan Bowman: Well, it's no good standing here complaining about it; there's work to be done.

Mrs Bowman: [*A little way from the microphone, to give the impression that she is the other side of the 'room*] Dan, I've brought your sandwiches and your flask.

Dan Bowman: Hallo love, you think of everything, don't you! Here, you've been crying. What's up, love?

Mrs Bowman: Oh it's nothing, Dan.

Dan Bowman: Now come on, love, out with it. Something's upset you. You can't keep things from me. Come on, what's wrong, lass?

Mrs Bowman: Well, it's young Diane. Mrs W. saw her coming out of the country club last night with Paul Black.

Dan Bowman: Paul Black? His divorce isn't through yet. [*Pause*] Are you sure it was our Diane?

Mrs Bowman: Well, Mrs W. said she saw her.

Dan Bowman: He's no good, Gladys. Where does he get his money from? That's what I'd like to know. I don't like it, Gladys. Oh no, I can't believe our Diane would go out with the likes of him.

[**Tony** *sitting against the studio wall and following the programme in his script, assumes an expression which says he knows better about Dan Bowman's daughter*]

Dan Bowman: There's plenty of decent lads in the village. I can't believe it.

Mrs Bowman: Well it's true, Dan. Joshua saw her as well.

Dan Bowman: That old scallywag, you can't believe anything he says.

[**Tony,** *still seated, reacts with mock outrage*]

Mrs Bowman: Well here he comes now, with his dog. You can ask him yourself.

George: Over here, Joshua!

[**Tony** *walks to the microphone, dressed for the part in a* *battered old hat, old coat, corduroys with a strap above the knees, and a knobbly stick under his arms*]

Tony: [*Singing, with Suffolk accent*] I've got mangel wurzels in my garden, I've got mangel wurzels in my shed ... I've got mangel wurzels in my bathroom, and a mangel wurzel for a head.

[*The rest of the cast is puzzled by this and look at their scripts. The* **actor** *impersonating a dog comes to the microphone yapping and snarling*]

Actor: [*Excitedly*] Yap, yap!

Tony: Down boy, get down, down.

Actor: Yap, yap, yap yap!

Tony: Get down, back you black-hearted creature, get down.

Actor: [*Snarling ferociously*] Grrrr!

Tony: Get down afore I fetches my stick across you. [**Tony** *and the* **actor** *are ready to have a go at each other*] Go on, lie down there.

[*The* **producer** *waves frantically at* **Tony,** *who points to the dog and mouths 'It's him'*]

George: Hallo Joshua, you old rascal!

Tony: Hallo George, me old pal, me old beauty, me old darling!

Dan Bowman: Joshua, I want a word with you.

Tony: Well dang my breeches, if you don't all a-look all worried like.

Actor: Grrrr...!

Tony: Get down, be quiet. [*He threatens the* **actor** *with a backhander*] What be the trouble then, Dan, me old pal, me old beauty? Has the blight been at your turnips again?

Dan Bowman: No, it's not that, Joshua.

Tony: Ah, then it's the kale up in North Meadow, it's gone to seed. I told 'ee to get it in last week, didn't I? But you wouldn't listen to old Joshua, no – no one listens to old Joshua. But he knows, old Joshua, he knows.

Actor: Yap, yap, grrrr. . . !

Tony: I'm warning you! [*He prods the* **actor** *with his stick*] One more yap out of you and you get this down your throat.

[**Tony** *prods the* **actor** *again, hurting him this time, and the* **actor** *pushes* **Tony.** **Tony** *is just going to wallop him with the stick, when* **Dan Bowman** *signals them to stop it, and* **Gladys** *nudges* **Dan** *with her elbow to get on with it. He looks at his script to find the place*]

Dan Bowman: Er . . . yes . . . er, no it's not the kale either, I got that in during the spell of fine weather last weekend.

Tony: Good, good, I'm glad to hear that, Dan, me old pal, me old beauty. Then what be a-bothering you then?

Dan Bowman: It's my daughter Diane.

Tony: Ah, then you've heard about that no good city slicker Paul Black.

Dan Bowman: Then it's true.

Tony: Aaah, of course it be true. I've been a-seeing of them with my own eyes. Coming out of the Turk's Head they was. A-giggling and a-cuddling and a-kissing . . .

Mrs Bowman: Oh Dan!

Dan Bowman: Steady, love.

Tony: Ah . . . but that aint be the worst of it.

Dan Bowman: What happened, Joshua?

Tony: I'm a-going to tell you what happened. I'm a-going to tell you what I saw with me own eyes.

Mrs Bowman: What did you see, Joshua?

Tony: I'm a-going to tell you what I saw.

Dan Bowman: Well come on, out with it man. What did you see?

Mrs Bowman: Yes, Joshua. What did you see our daughter and this man get up to?

Tony: All right then . . . I'll tell you.

[*The signature tune of the programme begins – something similar to 'The Archers'*]

Announcer: You have been listening to 'The Bowmans', an everyday story of simple people. The News and Radio Newsreel follow in a few moments.

[*The* **producer** *indicates that they are off the air, and the actors relax. They turn on* **Tony**]

Dan Bowman: [*In his real voice*] What on earth do you think you're playing at? Are you trying to ruin the programme?

Tony: It wasn't my fault. It was him, the dog, barking where he wasn't supposed to. He was trying to drown me. I know what he's up to.

Actor: I did not. I barked where I was supposed to bark.

Tony: You did not. It's got down here three yelps and a growl. You were a-barking and a-snarling all over the place. I've never seen such a disgraceful exhibition of drunkenness in the whole of my professional career.

Mrs Bowman: [*In her real, very educated, voice*] Well you shouldn't have poked him with that stick.

Tony: Would you kindly keep out of this, madam? I am the oldest member of the community. Let's have a little respect.

Mrs Bowman: You may be the oldest member of the village, Mr Hancock, but you are not the oldest member of this cast. Dan and I . . . [*She corrects herself*] Mr Osmington and I were the two originals. You were brought in after, and you can be taken out.

Tony: What do you mean by that? I've been in this show for five years; I get more fan mail than all the rest of you put together. Twenty million people gather round their radio sets at a quarter to seven every night, just waiting to have a giggle at the antics old Joshua gets up to. I carry this programme. It's only me and my bits of homespun philosophy, and my jokes, and my little rhymes, that's what keeps them glued to the set, mate, that's what they're waiting for. Not you moaning all round the house about the weather and your daughter and your rock cakes. Say nothing – here comes the producer.

[*The* **producer** *has left the control room and comes into the studio*]

Tony: Hallo Ronnie, another good'un, eh?

Producer: It was not a good one. You practically ruined the whole of the last five minutes.

Tony: Who, me?

Producer: You were putting bits in all over the place, and what do you mean by coming on singing that stupid song about mangel wurzels? That wasn't in the script.

Tony: I know it wasn't. I made it up.

Producer: You have no right to put bits in.

All: Quite right. Yes.

Tony: I portray the character as I see him. That's the sort of song he would sing. And I thought as he'd just emerged from the Turk's Head, it seemed quite reasonable to assume he would be singing. It's him who messed it up. [*He* *points to the* **actor**] Fido here.

Actor: How dare you! I may tell you that I'm one of the finest dog impersonators in the country.

Tony: You are supposed to be my obedient dog, you're supposed to do as you're told. Instead of that, you yap around me feet all the time I'm talking. I'll get the scriptwriter to have you gored by a bull or something, get an alsation in. Oh, I'm surrounded by amateurs.

[There is an uproar from the other actors]

Producer: All right, all right, stop quarelling. Now, here you are, here are the scripts for Monday evening.

[He hands a script to each of the cast, and they begin to look through it]

Tony: Ah yes, we'll find out what old Joshua saw outside the Turks Head. *[He reads the first page, and starts to laugh]* Oooh, oh dear oh dear! Fancy that! This is your daughter for you. Very good. *[He flips through the script]* What's this? Joshua falls in the threshing machine?

Producer: Oh yes, I've been meaning to have a word with you about that.

Tony: I should think so too.

Producer: He falls in the machine and is rushed off to hospital.

Tony: Oh. I see. A nice touch of human interest. Yes, old Joshua in hospital, what a good idea. I've got it – I'm on the danger list ... hovering between life and death. Twenty million people crying their eyes out, slowly he pulls through, courageous old Joshua, jokes with the doctors, his first day up, chasing the nurses round the ward, until six months later he emerges triumphant from the hospital, stronger than ever.

Producer: Well, not exactly. He dies on Tuesday night.

Tony: He dies?

Producer: Without regaining consciousness.

Tony: Have you gone raving mad? You seriously imagine the public are going to stand for this? You'll have a howling mob outside Broadcasting House hurling bricks through the windows.

Producer: I'm sorry, the decision has been taken. We're killing you off on Tuesday night.

Tony: But you can't kill off the most popular character in the whole programme. It's ridiculous. If you want to economize why don't you put *him* to sleep?

[*He indicates the dog actor*]

Actor: You can't get rid of me. I'm not just a dog, I'm the whole farmyard.

[*He does a quick medley of animal impressions*]

Producer: Yes, all right Harold, we're not getting rid of you. I'm sorry Mr Hancock, it's not a question of economy. Our audience research has found that the character of Joshua is falling off alarmingly in popularity.

Tony: Oh this is nonsense. I've never been so popular. Look at last year when I proposed to Mrs W. and she turned me down. I had three hundred and thirty-two proposals of marriage in the next post. And when I had that cough – fourteen gallons of lung syrup turned up. I am a real person to the listening public, I'm one of the family, they'll go beserk if I snuff it.

Dan Bowman: I doubt that very much. Miss Beaumont and I are the mainstay of this programme.

Tony: Well I'm not standing for this. I'm going straight to the top.

Producer: My instructions have come from the top.

Tony: Oh. Well it's the scriptwriters. They don't know what they're doing. They've made me far too unsympathetic. Last week I kicked the dog three times.

Producer: That wasn't in the script.

Tony: Well no. But he asked for it, shoving in yaps where there weren't any.

Producer: Yes that's another thing, your acting.

Tony: [*Defiantly*] And what is wrong with my acting?

Producer: You're erratic. We never know from show to show what sort of performance to expect.

Tony: Really. Don't you think these things, if to be said at all, should be said in the privacy of your office, and not in front of this crowd of gaping village idiots?

Producer: You asked for this. People have begun to notice your accent.

Tony: My accent is perfect. I spent six months in Somerset on a cider farm perfecting it.

Producer: It's never the same two performances running. Sometimes it's Somerset, sometimes it's Suffolk, a bit of Welsh, Birmingham, and last week I could swear we had a bit of Robert Newton in there. It's just not good enough. It completely destroys the illusion we are trying to build up. Who can believe in a character who indulges in these . . . these vocal gymnastics?

Tony: Vocal gymnastics? You're going too far, sir.

Producer: And these ridiculous clothes you wear. This is a radio show.

Tony: I wear these clothes to get the feeling of the part. Of course if you're completely ignorant of the Stanislavsky school of acting, I'm obviously wasting my time with this load of tat.

Producer: We don't want method actors in here.

Tony: I'm not a method actor. I don't just rush around the studio scratching myself. What do you know about it anyway? You come in here, an ex-sound mixer from Sports Report, telling me about acting. This is very nefarious, my good man. I warn you, if this is not put right over the weekend, I shan't be here on Monday for the *coup de grâce.*

Producer: We've thought of that possibility. We have an alternative script ready. So you can either go now and die over the weekend, or come in on Monday and get an extra day's pay.

Tony: [**Tony** *thinks about it*] I see. That's the way things are shaping, is it? As my landlady is pressing for rent, I shall be here on Monday for the threshing machine. But you haven't heard the last of this. Good day to you. [*As he passes the* **dog actor** *he addresses him*] And if you start yapping round my bedside I won't be too weak to fetch you a vicious blow with my stick. [*He opens the door, but then turns back to the assembled cast*] Untutored hams!

[*He slams the door behind him*]

2   The radio studio, on the following Monday

Again we see the 'On the Air' sign. It is towards the end of the next episode, and the cast are gathered around the microphone as before, with their scripts in their hands.

Dan Bowman: How is he, doctor?

Doctor: I'm sorry, Mr Bowman.

Mrs Bowman: You mean, there's no chance?

Doctor: I'm sorry. We've done all we can.

George: Poor old Joshua.

Fred: I think he's trying to say something.

Dan Bowman: What is it, Joshua old son?

[**Tony** *groans weakly*]

Mrs Bowman: We're here, Joshua. Your friends are here.

Tony: [*Groaning*] Gladys. Dan. I'm going.

Dan Bowman: No you're not, Joshua. You'll pull through. You'll soon be back at Brook Farm your old cheerful self again.

[**Tony** *coughs, and groans some more*]

Tony: [*Speaking with a Suffolk accent*] No, no, Dan, me old pal, me old beauty. The plough of time has come to the end of its furrow. [*He changes to a Scottish accent*] It's harvest time and the great farmer [*Now with a Welsh accent*] has come to gather me in, you see. [*As Robert Newton*] Aha Dan lad, I'll be in Valhalla on the noon tide . . . Ahaha.

[*He is nudged by the other actors, groans weakly, and continues in a variety of accents*]

Tony: I'm sinking . . . it won't be long now. I'm going. When you get your beetroots in, will you think of me? I'm going.

[*He does a big death scene with ridiculously exaggerated strangulation sounds and groans*]

Mrs Bowman: Er . . . I think he's gone, Dan.

Tony: [*Groaning loudly*] I'm going, I'm going. Goodbye Dan. Goodbye Gladys. Goodbye Fred, goodbye George. There's only one thing I'd like to ask before I go. Me last wish, me last wish. I'd like my dear old dog to be buried alongside of me.

[*He groans, and dies again, making another big performance of it*]

Mrs Bowman: I think . . . I think he's gone, Dan.

Diane: [*Coming to the microphone*] Mother . . . Father, am I too late?

Dan Bowman: I'm afraid you are, Diane. His poor old tired heart has finally stopped. He's gone to a better place for a long deserved rest.

[**Tony** *groans, and then coughs. The other actors try to push him away from the microphone, but he fights his way back*]

Tony: I'm still here, haven't gone yet. But I'm going. I'm going. Is that you Diane? Come to see old Joshua off on the long journey, have you? [*He coughs*] I'm going.

[*He groans again*]

Dan Bowman: Er . . . we'd better be getting back to the farm. There's nothing more we can do here with old Joshua . . . *dead!*

[**Tony** *tries to get in again, but they stand in front of him and stop him getting to the microphone. He dodges about, but they dodge with him and successfully bar his way. While the struggle goes on, the following dialogue takes place*]

Mrs Bowman: So he's gone. Dear kind-hearted old Joshua has gone.

Dan Bowman: The best friend a man ever had. Although he's gone, he'll always be with us.

[**Tony** *again attempts to get to the microphone. The* **producer,** *who has come into the studio in his shirtsleeves, tries to stop him.* **George** *covers the mike with his hands as*

Tony *approaches, and between them they manage to push him out again]*

Mrs Bowman: *[Beginning to cry]* Poor old Joshua.

Dan Bowman: Come on love, he wouldn't want us to stand here crying over him. Let's go home.

*[By now the **producer** has his arm round **Tony's** neck and his hand over his mouth to ensure that he says nothing more. **Tony** is struggling to get free and, as the signature tune comes in, he bites the **producer's** hand.]*

Announcer: You have been listening to 'The Bowmans', an everyday story of simple people. The News and Radio Newsreel follow in a few moments.

*[The actors all turn on **Tony** as soon as they are off the air. The **producer** is in obvious pain from **Tony's** bite]*

Dan Bowman: *[To **Tony**]* My word, you made a meal of that, didn't you?

Mrs Bowman: Disgusting performance.

Producer: This is the last time you ever work on one of my programmes.

Tony: You weren't getting rid of me as easily as all that. If I was going to go, I was going in a blaze of glory. Hallo, what have we got here?

[They all turn to see a new actor who has come into the studio]

Producer: I'd like you all to meet Julian Court. Julian is joining the programme from tomorrow night. He plays Gregory Forrester, who buys old Joshua's farm.

Julian Court: How do you do. I'm looking forward to a long and happy association with all of you.

Tony: It won't be a long one, mate. As soon as you start getting popular they'll have you in the threshing machine like a shot.

Producer: Mr Hancock, there's nothing more for you to do here. Would you be so good as to leave the studio?

Tony: With the greatest of pleasure.

Producer: Here's your money.

[*He hands* **Tony** *an envelope.* **Tony** *opens it*]

Tony: There's generosity for you. The golden handshake. Four pounds, twelve shillings and sixpence. Not even a week's wages.

Producer: They are Equity rates. One day's pay. Good afternoon.

[**Tony** *goes to the studio door, but then turns back*]

Tony: You'll regret this. You don't know what a little gem you had in me. I'm on me own now, I'll show you. It was only this hotchpotch of rural beatniks that have been holding me back. I'll get the chance to do some real acting for a change now. Good day to you.

[*He slams the door as he leaves. The* **producer** *starts introducing the new member of the cast*]

Producer: This is Windthrift Osmington.

[**Julian Court** *shakes hands with* **Dan Bowman**]

Producer: Celia Beaumont.

[*He shakes hands with* **Mrs Bowman,** *and moves on to the next actor*]

3   The stage of a small, provincial theatre

Auditions are taking place for a proposed production of 'Hamlet'. An **actor** *is just finishing the famous soliloquy from that play, and he is standing in a pool of light – the stage all round him is in darkness. A* **voice** *from the darkness interrupts him before he has finished.*

Voice: Thank you very much. We'll let you know. Next.

Actor: But I hadn't finished yet.

Voice: That's quite enough for us to judge. Thank you.

Actor: I have some more . . .

Voice: That's quite all right, we know what you can do. Next please.

[*The* **actor** *walks off, and* **Tony** *comes on. He puts down the case which he is carrying and peers out into the blackness, shielding his eyes from the footlights*]

Tony: Hancock. Anthony Hancock. Joshua in *The Bowmans*, an everyday story of simple people.

Voice: Thank you, carry on.

Tony: Yes, er . . . what would you like to hear?

Voice: Well if it's all the same to you we'd like to hear the part you came to audition for.

Tony: Yes, well I don't know very much about it, you see. I was in the coffee bar, I may be a little rusty . . .

Voice: Yes, carry on.

Tony: I don't normally do auditions, you know.

Voice: That's all right, carry on.

[**Tony** *leans over and opens his case. He takes out a wig, and puts it on*]

Voice: We don't need any props.

Tony: I thought it might add to the charm of the thing, give you some idea of how I'm going to interpret the role.

Voice: We are familiar with the costumes of the piece, just get on with the reading.

Tony: [*Taking off the wig*] Certainly, I do beg your pardon. It's a long time since I did an audition.

Voice: So you said. Now do hurry, come along please, we do have other people waiting.

Tony: Yes, quite. [*He clears his throat*] Hush, what light from yonder window breaks? 'Tis Juliet, and the sun is in the West . . .

Voice: Mr Hancock, the play is *Hamlet.*

Tony: *Hamlet?* Is it? I was distinctly told *The Merchant of Vienna.* I'm terribly sorry. *Hamlet* is a different cup of tea, of course. Which interpretation do you fancy?

Voice: We just want the words, loud and clear. This is a British Arts Council tour of Tanganyika, I'm sure they won't worry about the interpretation.

Tony: Tanganyika. I wasn't told that.

Voice: Do you want the part or not?

Tony: It's a few weeks in the sun, I suppose. What's the money like?

Voice: Let's wait and see whether you are right for the part, shall we?

Tony: Well I don't want to waste my time. I was clearing a fair whack at the BBC. I don't really want to drop below that.

Voice: [*Angrily*] Are you going to give us a reading or not?

Tony: Yes. [*He clears his throat, and then speaks in Joshua's voice*] To be or not to be, that be the question . . . whether 'tis nobler in the mind to suffer the slings and arrows of outrageous fortune . . .

Voice: Next.

Tony: Or to take arms . . . eh?

Voice: I said Tanganyika, not Norfolk. We'll let you know later.

Tony: Let me know later? I'm sorry, but that is not good enough.

Voice: All right. We'll let you know now. No. Next.

Tony: I feel I must remind you, young man, you are not dealing with any old yobidehoy, you are dealing with an actor of some merit. I just gave you the voice that captivated twenty million listeners every night for five years.

Voice: We're not interested. Next please.

Tony: I warn you, the Tanganyikans aren't going to like this. I am very highly thought of in Dar-es-Salaam. This is no way to keep the Commonwealth together. You will be playing to empty mud huts, my man. There are other managements, you know. I shall offer my services to those who appreciate the talents of a true artiste.

4   A film studio

A film crew are on the camera, waiting for their instructions from the **director.**

Director: Action!

[*The camera tracks in and we see the set. There is a lovely girl in a crinoline, powdered wig, carrying a black mask on the end of a stick.* **Tony** *enters, dressed in the Rupert of Schleswig Holstein full dress uniform with monocle. He* *sweeps his cloak in greeting and goes up to the girl. He clicks to attention and then kisses her hand. They sink down together on to a plush divan and she caresses his cheek*]

Announcer: [*Out of shot*] What has he got that other men haven't?

[**Tony** *brings a tin of pilchards out from under his cloak. The camera closes in on the tin. The girl gasps in pleasure as he shows it to her. She throws her arms round him and strokes his cheek*]

Announcer: Yes, Grimsby Pilchards, sought after by ladies of quality since 1811.

[*We see* **Tony** *looking at the camera over the girl's shoulder. He smirks and holds up the tin*]

Announcer: Grimsby Pilchards, twopence off for a trial offer.

[*We fade out, and fade up a country scene.* **Tony** *emerges from a tent, dressed as Napoleon, with his hand inside his tunic. He rubs his stomach with his free hand*]

Announcer: [*Out of shot*] Yes, Napoleon has every right to rub his tummy, he has just had a delicious meal of . . .

[**Tony** *brings his hand out of his tunic, to reveal a tin of Grimsby Pilchards. A girl, dressed as Josephine, runs up to him, throws her arms around him and strokes his cheek*]

Announcer: . . . Grimsby Pilchards, the food of Emperors.

[*We see a close up of* **Tony** *looking at the camera over Josephine's shoulders. He smirks and holds up the tin*]

Announcer: Grimsby Pilchards for men. Fourpence off for a trial offer.

[*We fade out again, and fade up a dance hall.* **Tony,** *in full* *evening dress, walks up to a girl who is in dance championships dress. He asks the girl to dance, but she shakes her head and dances off with a good looking boy.* **Tony** *gloomily looks after them, and then brightens up as he has an idea. He sits down and takes from his tails a tin of pilchards. He opens them with a tin opener, takes a fork and spears a bit, whereupon he is surrounded by beautiful girls all smiling at him and stroking his cheek. He smiles cockily]*

Announcer: *[Out of shot]* Yes, you're never alone with a pilchard.

*[***Tony*** *now has a girl on each knee and another couple hanging around his neck stroking his hair and cheek. He smirks and holds up the tin]*

Announcer: Grimsby Pilchards, sixpence off a trial offer.

[We see a shot of a graph marked 'Grimsby Pilchards Sales Campaign' with a line going straight across it. A hand comes in and draws a line downwards]

5   The interior of Tony's flat

Tony *enters, and takes off his hat and coat. He slings them away, takes off his jacket and slings that away, then collapses on the bed. He is very despondent.*

Tony: Fools! What a liberty, giving me the push. Best advert they've ever had. They can't blame me for what's inside the tin. I told them it was the tomato sauce that's turning people off. And they should have taken the heads off. Very unnerving to open a tin and see six heads staring up at you. But no, they have to have a scapegoat, go on, blame it on the artist. When anything goes wrong, kick the actor out. Oh, show business is being run by idiots these days. No men of vision left. Oh for the days of the actor manager, my own theatre and that [*He puts his thumb on his nose*] to all of them. They don't want talent these days. They just want a pretty face. [*There is a slight pause*] Not that I don't come under that category as well. I'm not a pretty boy, I agree . . . I'm more like Peter Finch. Oscar Wilde. [*In an exaggerated manner*] 'Parsley is ghastly'. Oh I think I'll turn acting in. Go and live on a barge. It's a facile life anyway. [*He puts on a posh voice*] 'Hallo, darling, caught the show last night, loved it, you were absolutely divine.' What a load of old rubbish. I'll be a missionary I think. Help the underprivileged people of the world. I hear it pays quite well too. Or should I just do away with myself . . .

[*There is a knock on the door.* **Tony** *goes and opens it. A* **postman** *is standing outside, carrying an enormous sack of letters*]

Postman: Mr Joshua Merryweather?

Tony: Who? Oh yes, yes of course.

[*The* **postman** *walks into the flat and heaves the sack off his shoulder and on to the floor*]

Postman: You caused a bit of a stink dying last night, didn't you?

Tony: Last night?

Postman: Yes, on the old Bowmans programme. My old woman was very cut up about it, you know.

Tony: That was two weeks ago.

Postman: No, last night. I heard it. Didn't you see the newspapers today? All over the front pages.

Tony: Of course, the programme is recorded in advance. It didn't go out till last night.

Postman: That's what I said. You've upset the whole

country you have. [*He points to the sack*] Look at that. Letters of protest, I shouldn't wonder. They're all up in arms about it. It's going to cost you a pretty penny to answer all those.

[*He goes out*]

Tony: They've all gone mad!

[*There is another knock on the door.* **Tony** *opens it, to find a* **porter** *standing there with two large wreaths*]

Porter: Mrs Joshua Merryweather, please.

Tony: Mrs . . .?

Porter: These floral tributes have been sent by sympathetic people throughout the country on the sad occasion of her husband's death.

[*The* **porter** *walks to the table, claps his hands, and half a dozen* **pageboys** *come in, all carrying wreaths and great bunches of flowers. They put them down*]

Porter: Ah, it's going to be a lovely funeral.

Tony: [*In disbelief*] This is madness!

Porter: There's more to come; from my establishment alone there's another six vanloads. I must say we were all very upset to hear the news. Tell Mrs Merryweather our hearts are with her in her hour of sorrow.

Tony: Oh this is ridiculous! It's only a programme.

Porter: When is the funeral? We've all got our armbands on. Ah yes, a day of national mourning. Oh, and here's a little tribute from my good lady wife and myself. [*He hands* **Tony** *a little wreath and points to the card*] 'Joshua Merryweather. Only sleeping.' Well, I'd better get back and comfort my wife, she hasn't stopped crying since last night, and I expect you have got all the arrangements to see to. Good morning.

[*As he leaves a young* **reporter** *rushes in*]

Reporter: Mr Hancock. I'm Tim Walters of the *Evening Globe*. I want to do a follow up story on tonight's main headline.

Tony: What are you talking about?

Reporter: Haven't you seen the papers? Look.

[*He hands* **Tony** *a paper, and* **Tony** *reads the headlines*]

Tony: [*Reading*] 'Nation stunned by untimely demise of Joshua Merryweather. Thousands of listeners jam telephone lines to BBC.' [*He looks pleased*] Really?

Reporter: It's fantastic. You realize the BBC had five thousand complaints in an hour after last night's programme?

Tony: [*Beaming, but maintaining his modesty*] Get away. [*He reads again*] 'A BBC spokesman said last night . . . "we had no idea this character was so popular. The heads of department are meeting to review the situation."'

Reporter: Now look, Mr Hancock. My paper would like to do a regular feature every night called The Joshua Merryweather Column, philosophical advice to the lonely and the miserable. You know, the sort of thing you've been doing on the programme, the quaint corny up against the pig sty sort of stuff . . . comments on the political situation, anything. You don't have to write it, all we want is a picture of you at the top and the name and we're willing to pay you £5000 a year.

Tony: Isn't that marvellous! Four pounds twelve and six a day when you're alive, five thousand a year when you're dead.

6   A conference room in Broadcasting House

A few BBC officials are sitting round a large table, **Tony**
sweeps in and they immediately rise to greet him.

Head official: My dear sir, welcome back to Broadcasting
House.

[*Another official holds a chair out for* **Tony,** *who sits
down*]

Head official: Have a cigar.

[**Tony** *takes the cigar. All the others rush to light it for him,
but he deliberately lights it with his own lighter*]

Head official: Well now, Mr Hancock, I'm sure that we
won't have any difficulty with our little problem.

Tony: I'm sure we won't.

Head official: Yes quite. We've made tentative arrangements for the return of your character to the programme.
[*Turning to the* **producer**] Mr Ponsonby?

Producer: Well I think you're going to like this, Tony.
[*Pause*] Joshua has a twin brother, looks like him, all the
gestures exactly identical. He suddenly turns up at
Brookhampton, buys his brother's old farm and sets up in
residence exactly as before.

Tony: How very ingenious.

Head official: You like it?

Tony: Yes, I think it's a very, very, very good idea.

[*They all beam at each other, relieved*]

Tony: There's only one snag.

Head official: What?

Tony: I'm not doing it – [*He pauses*] unless . . .

Head official: Yes?

Tony: Unless you agree to my terms. Ten thousand a year, five-year contract, I get top billing, I'll write all me own scripts, and a free radio licence.

Head official: Write all your own scripts?

Tony: Yes. I'm not having any more of this disappearing in the threshing machine again. Good afternoon, gentlemen, I don't think there is anything else to discuss. Your humble servant.

[*He takes a little bow and exits*]

7   Inside a radio studio

The rest of the Bowmans cast and **Tony** *are standing around the microphone. All but* **Tony** *look very sullen. The 'On the Air' sign goes on, the* **producer** *signals, and the signature tune begins. The* **announcer** *steps up to the microphone.*

Announcer: We present Anthony Hancock as Old Ben Merryweather, in 'The Merryweathers', an everyday story of Old Ben Merryweather.

Actor: Good morning Ben. How are you today?

Tony: Oh, ahh, me old pal, me old beauty.

Actor: What's the weather going to be like today then, Ben?

Tony: Well, I seen a crow on the wing this morning, and he went round in three circles and flew off to the North, ah it'll be raining by lunchtime.

Actor: Oh look, coming across the fields. There be Dan Bowman, Mrs Bowman, their daughter Diane, and George and Fred his farmhands, the Squire and his wife, old Jim who owns the tobacconists, the Vicar, and the Manager of the Turk's Head. Half the village be coming across.

Tony: Dang me, they shouldn't be walking across that field.

Actor: Why not?

[The rest of the cast cry out in unison. This is followed by silence]

Tony: *[Flatly]* Oh dear, what a shame. They've all fallen down that disused mine shaft.

Actor: We'd better get them out.

Tony: No, no, there be no point. No, no, no, no. Three hundred foot deep it is. They'll all be splattered across the bottom. Ha, ha. Fill it in and forget about them. Put some of them wreaths we had left over from Joshua on top of them.

Actor: But that be half the village gone.

Tony: Ah, but we'll soon stock it up again, lad. I've got a lot of relatives knocking about. I reckon I can run this village on my own. *[He sings]* I've got mangel wurzels in my garden, I've got mangel wurzels in my shed ... I've got mangel wurzels in my bathroom, and a mangel wurzel for a head. *[Laughing merrily]* Ahaaa ... ha ... ha ...

*Judi Dench as Laura and Michael Williams as Mike Selway in
London Weekend Television's* A Fine Romance

A Fine Romance
Series 1, episode 1
Bob Larbey

First shown on London Weekend Television on 1 November 1981 (produced by Humphrey Barclay and directed by James Cellan-Jones)

Characters

Phil
Helen, his wife
Laura, Helen's sister
Mike Selway, a landscape gardener
Harry, a guest at Helen's party
Jean, another guest
Redheaded girl
Other party guests

A Fine Romance

---

1 Phil and Helen's bedroom

Like the rest of the house, the bedroom is modern and quite elegant. **Helen** *sits at her dressing table wearing Janet Reger underwear and a négligé. She is about thirty-two, very pretty and looks like a picture advertising an idealized woman in an idealized home. It is early evening.*

Her sister **Laura** *comes in.* **Laura** *is about six years older than* **Helen** *and quite without her looks.* **Laura** *wears a long party dress with a pinny over it.*

Laura: I've impaled about a thousand little sausages on little sticks. Is that OK?

Helen: Thanks Laura. You are a pet.

Laura: Yes. [*This is obviously a word she doesn't like*] Anything else?

Helen: No. People will be arriving in an hour or so. You just get yourself ready.

Laura: [*Taking off her pinny*] I *am* ready.

Helen: Oh.

Laura: Helen, this party – you and Phil aren't going to try to fix me up with somebody, are you?

Helen: Now when have we ever tried to do that?

Laura: All the time.

Helen: Well not this time. I promise.

[**Helen**'s *husband,* **Phil,** *comes in. He is a good-looking chap – about two years older than she*]

Phil: Well that's blown it. Vic's called off.

Laura: Who's Vic?

Phil: This fellow we wanted you to meet.

[**Laura** *looks accusingly at* **Helen,** *who looks daggers at* **Phil** *who catches on too late*]

Phil: Not that it matters. No he's just a bloke who was coming to the party. Nothing more to it than that. Certainly not. I'm floundering, aren't I?

Laura: You've drowned.

[**Phil** *smiles weakly and goes*]

Laura: You won't give up, will you?

Helen: I don't know why you get so stroppy about it. You're single. Now what is wrong with me inviting the odd single chap?

Laura: Because that's what they usually turn out to be – the 'odd' single chap.

Helen: That's not true.

Laura: [*Calming down*] No, it's not. I'm sorry. [*She smiles*] Mind you, there was that Danish dentist with the perfect teeth and the whip above his bed.

Helen: Mistake, granted. [*She has a second thought*] How did you get to know about the whip above his bed?

Laura: How do you think?

Helen: Oh.

Laura: Yes. Mind you, he was drunk.

Helen: Oh Laura, stop it. To hear you talk, anyone would think you looked like Whistler's Mother.

Laura: Well I'm not Jane Fonda, am I?

Helen: That's going to extremes.

Laura: True. She's older than I am.

Helen: In any case, there are plenty of qualities far more important than looks.

Laura: Tell me about them.

Helen: Well . . . intelligence. I've always envied you your intelligence – you know that. Dad used to say to me, 'Helen, you've got the beauty but your sister's got the brains.'

Laura: Don't you dare stand there in your Janet Reger underwear and tell me I'm cleverer than you are!

Helen: Well you are.

Laura: Sometimes I don't want to be cleverer than you. *I* want to stand there in Janet Reger underwear!

Helen: [*Lost*] Well buy some.

Laura: Oh God, that's not it! [*She goes, passing* **Phil** *on his way back in. She views him suspiciously*] Something?

Phil: Nothing. Nothing. [**Laura** *goes*] I've cracked it. I'll ask Mike.

Helen: Mike?

Phil: Yes.

Helen: [*Incredulously*] Mike?

Phil: Yes. What's wrong with Mike?

Helen: Well, it's not exactly that anything's wrong with Mike. There's just nothing really right with him.

Phil: Look at it this way. It's the eleventh hour – he's single and so far as I know he's warm and breathing – that's what's right with him.

2   Mike's office

This is actually a large garden shed with windows. An old desk and two chairs form a small clearing in a jungle of well-used gardening equipment. There is a filing cabinet – some of its drawers open and bulging with papers.

The telephone on the desk is ringing. The door half opens. It will only half open because a large sack of peat has fallen down. **Mike Selway** *forces his way in. He is about forty – shortish and very unspectacular in appearance. He wears dungarees and an open-necked shirt. He makes his way through the shambles to the telephone and answers it.*

Mike: Selway Garden Landscaping. Mike Selway speaking. This is a recorded message. Sorry we're closed but if you'd like to leave your name and . . . Oh, Phil. Hello. No, I realize I'm not an answering machine, but I'm down in the Yellow Pages as having one and mine's on the blink. Anyway, what can I do for you? A party? [*On the word,* **Mike** *starts to look like a cornered rabbit. He shakes his head*] Tonight? [*With feigned enthusiasm*] Yes, I'd love to. Great. Smashing. No, try and keep me away, mate! Yes, I'll get cleaned up and be right over. Look forward to it. See you, Phil. [*He puts the phone down with an air of despair*] You don't want to go but you say you do.

[*He thumps the desk and a pile of papers flutter to the floor*]

3   Phil and Helen's lounge

The party is in its early, quiet stages. About twelve people have arrived so far and are standing around in little groups, chatting with their drinks in hand.

   Laura *is managing to keep on the fringe of things by walking* *about with a plate of sausages on sticks.* **Helen** *breaks away from a group and comes over to her.*

Helen: Laura!

Laura: What?

Helen: Come on – circulate!

Laura: I am. I'm going round and round trying to shift these sausages.

Helen: You do not meet people by giving them sausages! [*She propels* **Laura** *to a couple talking –* **Harry** *and* **Jean**] Jean – Harry. I don't think you know my sister, Laura.

Jean: Hallo.

Harry: [*Making it sound like an ultimate truth*] So you're Laura!

[*She is well aware that this is not a sparkling opening. They wait, but nothing happens*]

Harry: We were just discussing death.

Laura: Oh. Whose?

Harry: Oh nobody's in particular. Just death. Big D.

Jean: Harry was just saying . . . it's so awfully inevitable, isn't it?

Laura: There's no arguing with that.

Harry: And when all's said and done what's it all about?

Laura: [*Interrupting*] It keeps undertakers in business, I suppose.

Harry: No, I mean, what is life actually for? Big L.

Laura: I'm sorry. I thought you were talking about Big D.

Jean: Yes, but Harry was relating death to life. He finds the two things so . . . related, you see.

Laura: There's no arguing with that either.

Harry: No, no – you don't have to be polite. Come on – give me an argument on this.

[**Laura** *offers the plate of sausages –* **Harry** *and* **Jean** *both take one*]

Laura: Well, you're both eating a dead pig – right?

[*They freeze,* **Harry** *in mid-bite, with a fixed smile.* **Helen** *pulls* **Laura** *away*]

Helen: Do excuse us. [*She moves* **Laura** *away*] Laura, do you practise conversation-killers like that?

Laura: I can't make small talk. I can't even make medium talk. Look, just let me potter about. I'll take the sausages round again and I promise I won't refer to them as dead pig. Would you like one?

Helen: No thanks.

[**Laura** *wanders off.* **Helen** *shakes her head and beckons to* **Phil.** *He comes over and they find a quiet corner of the room. They conduct their conversation with lots of outward nods and smiles as though they are not the host and hostess having one of 'those' conversations.*]

Helen: Look, Mike *is* coming, isn't he?

Phil: He said he was. Why?

Helen: Because Laura is wandering about making people nervous.

Phil: You make her sound like an escaped lunatic.

Helen: You know the next step. She'll hide in the kitchen and start washing up.

Phil: There isn't any to speak of yet.

Helen: She'll find some. Remember Christmas? Three hours she was in that kitchen. By the time I got her to come out she'd started to clean the windows.

Phil: You know, I'm not sure inviting Mike was such a good idea.

Helen: I never really thought it was.

Phil: No, I'm thinking of it from his point of view. I mean, look at it this way. You're a bachelor and you get invited to a party at the last minute. Now why do you come?

Helen: [*Curious*] I don't know. Why?

Phil: Basically in the hope of meeting a bit of spare – preferably a redhead with long legs and big green eyes – green for 'Go'.

Helen: You've never told me you have a thing about redheads.

Phil: Me? I was talking about Mike.

Helen: Is that why *you* used to go to parties?

Phil: No. I *like* parties. If you *like* parties, you're not fussy – anybody will do.

Helen: You met me at a party.

Phil: All I'm saying is that I'm not at all sure that Laura is Mike's cup of tea.

Helen: Really? Well he's hardly one of the world's top ten eligible bachelors, is he?

Phil: True.

Helen: [*Looking towards the door*] Well anyway, he'd better get here soon.

Phil: [*Looking towards* **Laura**] She's not heading for the kitchen, is she?

Helen: No, she's just dropped one of her contact lenses in someone's drink.

[**Helen** *hurries over.* **Laura** *is the centre of attraction as a crowd gathers to help retrieve the contact lens.* **Laura** *obviously wishes the floor would open up and swallow her*]

4   The street outside Phil and Helen's house

Mike *pulls up in his van. It is a Dormobile with sliding doors. The van has 'Selway Landscape Gardening' painted on its side. It is dirty and beaten up, and like* **Mike'***s office it is cluttered with all sorts of garden equipment. There is no proper passenger seat, but an old wicker armchair.*

   Mike, *now wearing a suit, switches off the engine. He checks his appearance in the driving mirror and grimaces. Then he sprays some 'Gold Spot' into his mouth and grimaces again.*

Mike: Right! [*But he does not move*] Why don't I go home? To what? [*Resolving*] OK. Get ready, world. Here I come! [*His resolution is marred because his door is stuck. He wrestles with it, then gives up, clambers across the wicker chair and gets out of the passenger door. He forces himself to walk very quickly along the road and up the path to* **Phil** *and* **Helen'***s house. He rings the bell and for one mad moment considers flight*] Too late!

   [*He fixes a smile on his face*]

5   The hall of Phil and Helen's house

More people have arrived by now. **Helen** *answers the door.*

Helen: Mike!

Mike: Rosemary!

Helen: Helen.

Mike: Helen. Of course. I know you're Helen. I don't know why I said 'Rosemary'. I don't even know a Rosemary.

Helen: No. Well come in.

Mike: Come in. Right. I'm in!

6 Phil and Helen's lounge

Mike *comes in. His nerves are now displaying themselves as an awful, fixed cheerfulness which makes him look slightly crazed.* **Phil** *comes through the crowd.*

Phil: Good to see you, Mike. Come and have a sausage.

[**Helen** *winces at the subtlety. Slightly bewildered,* **Mike** *is led through the crowd towards* **Laura,** *who is standing rather aimlessly on the fringe of a conversation.* **Laura** *sees them coming and tries to escape but* **Helen** *and* **Phil** *head her off expertly*]

Helen: Laura – come and meet Mike.

Mike: Hallo. Hallo.

Laura: [*Put off by his awful fixed grin*] Hallo.

[*Nothing follows*]

Helen: Laura's my sister.

Mike: So . . .

[*He can't think of anything else, so his awful grin just gets slightly bigger*]

Phil: What are you drinking, Mike?

Mike: Please.

[**Phil** *shrugs and goes to get him a drink. As the others show no signs of an opening conversational gambit.* **Helen** *searches for one*]

Helen: Laura's a linguist.

Mike: Oh?

Laura: Somewhat.

Mike: Bon.

Laura: Oui.

[*This is a bad word. It puts the thought into* **Mike's** *head*]

Mike: Excuse me. Loo.

[*He hurries away*]

Laura: Helen, why on earth do you keep trying to fix me up when I don't want you to?

Helen: Now why on earth should you think that?

Laura: He comes through the door. You grab him, plough through the crowd like a harvester through a field of corn and introduce him to *me*, that's why!

Helen: I just want you to be as happy as Phil and me.

Laura: Helen, life is not *like* you and Phil.

Helen: At least try.

Laura: With him?

Helen: He's not that awful.

Laura: No? So far as I can see, he's a monosyllabic dwarf with a fixed grin and a weak bladder!

7   The upstairs loo

Mike *sits on the loo. He is fully dressed and the lid is down. On the wall is a giant crossword and* **Mike** *is applying himself to it.*

Mike: [*Reading*]I am alone the villain of the 'something'. Enobarbus in *Antony and Cleopatra*. [*Musing*] I am alone the villain of the . . . five letters . . . of the . . . Piece! [*He writes in 'Piece'. Then he looks again*] No, that's wrong. That makes Twelve Down 'Policp'. 'Earth'. That's it. 'I am alone the villain of the earth'.

[*He tries to alter 'Piece' to 'Earth' but is too heavy-handed with his pen. It goes through the crossword and makes a nasty tear; he licks his finger and tries to stick the tear back together again, but not very successfully. He looks at his watch*]

Mike: [*Singing tunelessly*] I don't want to go downstairs. I don't want to go downstairs ...

8   The landing outside the loo

Phil *comes upstairs, he hears the singing from the loo and listens more closely.*

Phil: Mike?

[*The singing is changed rapidly to 'I don't want to see the world on fire'*]

Phil: Mike?

Mike: Yes?

Phil: You all right? You've been in there half an hour.

Mike: Fine. [*We hear the loo flushing, then* **Mike** *comes out*] Bit of a stomach upset. Too much to drink, I expect.

Phil: You haven't drunk anything yet. Now come down and talk to Laura.

Mike: Who's Laura?

Phil: Laura! Helen's sister. You met her.

Mike: [*Unenthusiastically*] Oh. Yes.

Phil: She's an awfully nice girl.

Mike: Yes, I'm sure she is.

Phil: Awfully interesting too.

Mike: To be honest, Phil, she's not really my type.

Phil: You don't know that. Laura has qualities which ... [*Pause*] Well blimey, she's better than nothing, isn't she?

9 Phil and Helen's lounge

Laura *has been stopped by* **Helen** *as she is en route to the kitchen with a tray of dirty glasses.*

Helen: I know Mike may not be exactly your type . . .

Laura: He's not anybody's type! I mean, that smile – all fixed and glassy. He looked like something from Madame Tussaud's!

Helen: He's shy. *You're* shy. You should understand that.

Laura: Of course I understand it, but I don't have to like it. I don't like looking at a reflection of me. Look, I'll wash up.

Helen: No. There he is now. Look.

[**Mike** *comes downstairs with* **Phil**]

Laura: Phil must have broken the door of the loo.

Helen: Laura! Oh Mike, there you are!

Mike: Yes.

Laura: Will you please utter more than one syllable!

Mike: [*Taken aback*] Yes. All right.

Laura: Thank you.

Helen: Now why don't you two get yourselves a drink, sit down and have a nice chat?

Mike: No, well if Laura's going to wash up . . . [*He begins to edge away but* **Helen** *quickly takes the tray from* **Laura.** **Mike** *and* **Laura** *give in*] What would you like to drink?

Laura: Gin and tonic, please.

Mike: Right.

Phil: [*Quickly*] I'll get them.

[**Phil** *nips smartly off*]

Mike: [*To* **Laura**] Where would you like to sit?

Laura: On a seat?

Helen: There, there! Sit there!

[*They allow themselves to be almost put on a sofa.* **Laura** *looks from her eyeline to his*]

Laura: You're taller than I thought you were.

Mike: So are you.

[*This doesn't go down too well.* **Phil** *bustles up with two glasses of gin and an unopened bottle of tonic*]

Phil: There we are. [*He puts the drinks on a coffee table*] Right, that's you two fixed up.

[**Helen** *glares at him.* **Mike** *and* **Laura** *both look flatly at him*]

Phil: I didn't mean . . . Oh, blow it!

[*He rejoins the rest of the party.* **Helen** *gives them a smile of encouragement and does the same.*

Alone, **Mike** *and* **Laura** *smile bleakly at each other; they are striking no chorus at all*]

Laura: Let's have a drink.

[*She picks up the bottle of tonic*]

Mike: No, no, let me do that. [*He takes the bottle. He should have known better – the screw top is a tight one. He wrestles unsuccessfully, hating the inevitability of it all*] I need a cloth. A hankie!

[*He puts the bottle down and searches his pockets for a hankie.* **Laura** *has a go at the bottle and opens it. As she does so, she almost wishes she hadn't.* **Mike** *wishes she hadn't as well. He simply holds up his glass to allow her to* *pour the tonic in. She does, then adds tonic to her own. They don't bother with the 'Cheers', but sip silently]*

Laura: I think companionable silences are a myth.

Mike: I talk too *much* sometimes.

Laura: [*Unable to keep the sarcasm from her voice*] Really?

Mike: Yes. Particularly with strangers. I start talking without really knowing what I'm going to say, but I keep talking – then I start to hear the sound of my own voice as if it's echoing in a tunnel, but I keep talking. The last party I went to, I got onto a wall.

Laura: Not literally?

Mike: No. The subject of a wall I'd been putting up in this fellow's garden. I'm a landscape gardener, you see. Anyway, I got onto the subject of this wall and I couldn't get off it. The fellow kept changing his mind, you see. First of all he wanted Cotswold stone, then Derbyshire Stone, then he thought he'd have screen walling – during which time I was going slowly bananas. Well finally he settled for Cotswold, which of course needs to be laid in the half-bond manner. No, he didn't want that, so I said to him, 'Look, the half-bond manner is the only way . . . [**Mike** *tails off. This subject is not riveting* **Laura** *at all*] And I can hear the sound of my own voice in that tunnel again. You. Let's talk about you. Helen said you were a linguist.

Laura: Minor.

Mike: Oh. Surface work or at the coal face? [*This falls very flat*] Sorry. A minor linguist. And what do you do for a living?

Laura: Ling.

Mike: Sorry?

Laura: I translate things. It's all pretty boring.

Mike: Oh I'm sure it's not. What are you translating at the moment?

Laura: A German textbook about urinary infections.

Mike: Oh.

[*There is a silence*]

Laura: [*Desperately*] There's always sex.

[**Mike's** *mouth drops open*]

Laura: To talk about, I mean. That's always common ground.

Mike: Oh sure. Every party conversation gets round to it sooner or later.

Laura: Always.

[*But neither feels capable of opening the batting.* **Harry** *comes through the crowd with* **Jean** *in tow*]

Harry: [*To* **Laura**] Ah, there you are. I wanted to take you up on our discussion about death. You never really developed your argument.

Jean: Harry loves people to develop their argument.

Harry: So. How do you really feel about death?

Laura: At the moment, close to it. Excuse me.

[*She gets up and goes.* **Harry** *and* **Jean** *look put out and move away.* **Mike** *sits alone with his drink. An attractive* **Redheaded Girl** *comes and sits on the other end of the sofa. She smiles at* **Mike,** *who smiles back.* **Mike** *then looks away, obviously plucking up the nerve to make some approach*]

Mike: [*Finally*] Hi!

Girl: Yes I am.

[**Mike** *isn't sure what this means but guesses at something to do with drugs. This scares him and he slides right up to his end of the sofa*]

10   Phil and Helen's bedroom

Laura *has made a space on the bed on the far side of a heap of coats. She lies there reading a book she has picked up with no real interest. She hears the sound of voices approaching and is not pleased.*

Harry: [*Opening the door*] There's nothing *wrong* with animal instincts, Jean. After all, we *are* animals.

[**Laura** *drops the book, props herself on one elbow and talks into the pile of coats as though a man were there*]

Laura: Mike, stop it – there's somebody coming!

[**Harry** *and* **Jean** *stop at the doorway, properly embarrassed*]

Harry: Sorry!

Jean: Sorry!

Laura: Sorry!

[*They go quickly,* **Laura** *is pleased with her ploy, then remembers the name she used –* **Mike.** *She makes a face, then gives the coats a mock sexual look*] Oh Mike, you magnificent animal! Do you know what I want you to do now? I want you to undress me very slowly and whilst you're doing it I want . . . yes, I'll say it . . . I want you to drive me mad by talking about your bloody boring stone walls . . . [*This makes her laugh. She goes back to the book, but to her annoyance she hears footsteps and sees the handle of the door turning. This time she tries to pre-empt any entrance at all*]

Laura: [*As if in ectasy*] Oh Mike! Mike! Mike! Mike!

[*The door opens and* **Mike** *comes in*]

Mike: Yes?

Laura: Oh. Look, are you following me about?

Mike: That's the last thing I'd do.

Laura: Good.

Mike: Why were you saying 'Mike' like that?

Laura: Was I?

Mike: Yes. 'Mike! Mike! Mike!', you said.

Laura: If you must know, I was trying to keep people out – you know.

Mike: Oh I see. Why Mike though?

Laura: Don't read anything into it.

Mike: Difficult not to.

Laura: It's just the first name that came into my head. I mean – tonight – what's the first girl's name that would come into your head?

Mike: Helen?

Laura: Oh.

Mike: What are you doing up here anyway?

Laura: Taking sanctuary . . .

Mike: Me too. I was going to get on with the crossword in the loo, but somebody's in there.

Laura: Wait here if you like.

Mike: Thanks. [**Mike** *sits on the edge of the bed.* **Laura** *picks up her book and reads. A silence.* **Mike** *puts the alarm clock right*] This is daft. We're hiding from each other and here we are on the same bed.

[**Laura** *smiles ruefully*]

Laura: It's no good going down or we'll have Helen and Phil trying to glue us together again.

Mike: You get pretty hostile about that, don't you?

Laura: Don't you?

Mike: No. You can always live in hope, can't you? I mean, meeting women at my age . . . I don't know where there *are* any any more. I even went to an Over 25's Dance Night once, and I was the youngest one there. So if I'm asked, I come to parties. I hate parties but I come because sooner or later I might meet someone who's not just this lame dog that everyone's trying to palm off on me. [*Too late* **Mike** *realizes that this definition has included* **Laura.** *She glares*] I'm sorry. I didn't mean . . .

Laura: You big-head! Why do you think *you* get invited? Do you think people have got Jane Fonda staying with them for the weekend and say, 'Now, who can we invite for Jane? I know – of course! Mike!' – ?

Mike: If it was Jane Fonda I wouldn't mind.

Laura: She would.

Mike: Yes, but she can afford to be choosy.

Laura: And I can't?

Mike: I didn't say that. But be realistic. You're not as . . . you're hardly . . . well, you're older than Jane Fonda.

Laura: I'm not.

Mike: Look, I don't know how she got into the conversation. I'm talking about ordinary people and all I'm saying . . .

Laura: I know what you're saying. How old are you – fifty?

Mike: Forty-three.

Laura: Forty-three – you have about as much social grace

as one of your bits of stone and you've got the bloody
arrogance to expect to be fixed up with someone who isn't
as dull as you!

Mike: What about you? What gives you the right to be so
choosy?

Laura: Because I have the right! Just because I'm plain or
homely or downright ugly doesn't mean that I have to jump
at anything in trousers who bothers to say 'Hallo' to
me.

Mike: That's what *I* meant. Substitute 'skirt' for 'trousers'
and that's what *I* meant.

Laura: Oh. Yes, I see.

[*There is a silence. The door opens and* **Helen** *comes in*]

Helen: Laura, if you're hiding up here and . . . [*She stops.
What she sees is* **Laura** *lying on the bed and* **Mike** *sitting on
the bed*] Oh.

Mike: Look we're not . . .

Laura: [*Quickly*] Come on Helen – play the game!

Helen: Yes, of course. I had no idea. You carry on with what
you were doing . . . [*Correcting herself*] talking about. You
carry on.

[**Helen** *goes, looking pleased as Punch*]

Mike: Now why did you give your sister the idea that we
were in the bedroom together?

Laura: Well we are.

Mike: Ah, yes, it's hardly a romantic tryst though, is it? If
the loo hadn't been occupied, I'd have been in there doing
the crossword and you'd have been in here reading.

Laura: It's better for Helen to think she saw what she
thought she saw. It will make her whole evening.

Mike: She's very attractive, isn't she, Helen?

Laura: [*Shortly*] Yes.

Mike: [*Dutifully*] And so are you.

Laura: Oh come on!

Mike: No, in your own way . . .

[*He sees hostility rearing its head again and decides on a short cut with a sudden kiss. He leans over the coats all too suddenly and grabs* **Laura** *by the shoulders. As he transfers his weight she goes backwards and cracks her head on the bedhead and he hurts his groin on something under the coats*]

Laura: Oh!

Mike: Oww!

Laura: You berk, that was my head!

Mike: I'm sorry. Ooh! [*He finds the object that caused the pain – a solid briefcase*] Now why bring that to a party? And it would have poncy gold initials on it, wouldn't it? You all right?

Laura: Yes. What did you want to go and do that for?

Mike: Well we don't seem to be meeting about anything else. And at least . . . touching . . . well it gives you something to remember the day by, doesn't it? I mean, if I went to a party when I was a kid . . . well at least I didn't feel a total wash-out if I'd at least put my hand on a girl's knee.

[**Laura** *takes his hand and puts it on her knee – with no warmth at all*]

Laura: There. Your evening has not been a total wash-out.

[**Mike** *takes his hand off*]

Mike: That is the single most unromantic act I've ever seen in my life.

Laura: Second only to your adolescent attempt to fracture my skull.

[*There is a pause*]

Mike: We're wasting our time, aren't we?

Laura: I think we are. Let's go.

Mike: Where?

Laura: Home.

Mike: Oh. No. Thanks all the same but . . .

Laura: I'm not inviting you to my home. I just want to go home but I think we'd do best to leave together.

Mike: Why?

Laura: Because it's early and if either one of us tries to make it to the front door on his or her own . . .

Mike: [*Catching on*] Yes. 'Oh you're not going yet, surely? Have another drink.'

Laura: Exactly.

Mike: [*Getting off the bed*] Makes sense. Did you have a coat?

Laura: [*Picking up the briefcase*] No. Just a briefcase. [*They tidy themselves up*] Do you have false teeth?

Mike: No! Why?

Laura: Because when you kissed me I heard this strange clicking sound.

Mike: [*Sarcastically*] Must have been one of the bones in my surgical corset.

[*He opens the door. They both put on a happy face and leave*]

11   The street outside Phil and Helen's house

Mike *and* **Laura** *come out of the house with* **Helen** *and* **Phil** *seeing them off.*

Mike: Thanks for a lovely party. Goodnight.

Helen: Ring me Laura! Ring me!

Laura: Yes, all right. Goodnight.

Phil: Goodnight. Be good!

[**Mike** *puts his arm round* **Laura** *as they walk away*]

Helen: [*Pleased*] Well, well, well!

Phil: [*Surprised*] Well, well, well!

[*The* **Redhead** *appears in the doorway behind* **Phil** *and* **Helen**]

Girl: Phil! Come and dance with me!

Phil: You bet!

[*He goes.* **Helen** *closes the front door and follows, not liking his alacrity.* **Mike** *and* **Laura** *stop at his van*]

Laura: Well, we made it. Goodnight.

Mike: Let me give you a lift at least.

[**Laura** *looks askance at the van but shrugs.* **Mike** *opens the passenger door and she climbs in. She reaches to the wicker chair but sits in it gingerly.* **Mike** *goes round to his door, wrestles with it but fails to open it. He comes round to the passenger door and clambers over* **Laura**]

Mike: Sorry. [*He gets into the driver's seat*] Where to?

Laura: Fulham. Is it out of your way?

Mike: [*With no surprise at all*] Yes.

[**Mike** *starts the van and pulls away.* **Laura** *tips back in her chair but saves herself by grabbing the door handle*]

12   The street in front of a large block of flats

The van pulls up.

Mike: So.

Laura: So.

Mike: [*Looking at his watch*] It's still only half-past nine.

Laura: Doesn't time fly when you're having a rotten time?

Mike: Yes. Look, what about a curry?

Laura: Ugh! Chinese?

Mike: Hate it. Italian?

Laura: Where?

Mike: I don't know. We're just making noises, aren't we? Let's cut our losses.

Laura: Probably best. Goodbye Mike.

Mike: Goodbye, Laura.

[*She motions him not to get out. She gets out and goes towards the flats.* **Mike** *watches her, slowly getting the feeling that one of them should have tried harder. He resolves just as she reaches the doors of the flats. He tries to open his door but can't. By the time he gets out to the passenger door and up to the double doors of the flats,* **Laura** *has gone.* **Mike** *tries the double doors but they are of the automatic locking variety. He looks at all the little name-plates with bells by them but shrugs as he realizes he doesn't know* **Laura**'s *surname. He goes back to the van and unthinking tries to slide open his door. It glides easily back*]

Mike: Yes, you would open now, wouldn't you? You just would!

[*He gets in and slams the door. The handle falls off and he drives away*]

Derek Fowlds as Bernard Woolley (Jim's private secretary),
Paul Eddington as Jim Hacker and Nigel Hawthorne as Sir
Humphrey in Yes Minister. *(BBC copyright)*

Yes Minister
The Right to Know
Jonathan Lynn and Antony Jay

Characters

Jim Hacker, Minister for Administrative Affairs
Sir Humphrey Appleby, Permanent Under-Secretary of
  State in the Department of Administrative Affairs,
  known as the Permanent Secretary
Bernard, Jim's Principal Private Secretary
Sir Frederick, Permanent Secretary to the Foreign and
  Commonwealth Office (known as Jumbo)
Annie, Jim's wife
Lucy, Jim's daughter
Male Protester
Female Protester
Peter
Assistant
Protestors

Act, short for Act of Parliament

Assistant Secretary, fairly high-ranking official in a
government department. Only the Permanent Secretary,
Deputy Secretary and Under-secretary are more senior.

Department of Administrative Affairs, imaginary
ministry or department created to administer
government administration

Parliamentary Question, questions put by MPs to
ministers in the House of Commons

Permanent Under-secretary of State, also called
Permanent Secretary. The minister is the political and
temporary head of a government department, whereas
the Permanent Secretary the top civil servant and is a
permanent official.

Principal Private Secretary, (Chief Private Secretary),
a civil servant who works for the minister personally

Red boxes, secure boxes or cases in which ministers
carry state papers they must read

Yes Minister
The Right to Know

---

1   Sir Humphrey's office

Sir Humphrey *is working at his desk. There is a knock on the door, and* **Bernard** *puts his head round the door.* **Sir Humphrey** *beckons him in and, still working, points to a chair.* **Bernard** *sits down.*

Sir Humphrey: Good-morning, Bernard. Minister not in yet?

Bernard: Yes, Sir Humphrey. He's in his office having a meeting.

Sir Humphrey: What about?

Bernard: [*Evasively*] Nothing very important.

Sir Humphrey: I see. And what was that meeting in there yesterday?

Bernard: The Minister was just reviewing procedures for briefing him on answers to Parliamentary questions.

Sir Humphrey: But there were Principals present. And Assistant Secretaries, and other assorted underlings.

Bernard: Just the ones who actually supply him with the actual information, actually, Sir Humphrey.

Sir Humphrey: Bernard. This has to be stopped at once.

Bernard: Why?

Sir Humphrey: If he talks to the underlings he may learn things *we* don't know. Our whole position could be undermined.

Bernard: Why? If it increases our knowledge . . .

Sir Humphrey: [*Interrupting*] It is folly to increase your knowledge at the expense of your authority.

Bernard: Why?

Sir Humphrey: Bernard, please stop saying 'Why'.

Bernard: Why? . . . Um, I mean, could you develop that point, please?

[**Sir Humphrey** *sighs*]

Sir Humphrey: Would you say that the Minister is starting to run the Department?

Bernard: Oh, yes indeed, actually, things are going pretty well, actually.

Sir Humphrey: No Bernard, when a Minister actually starts to run his Department things are not going pretty well, actually. They are actually going pretty badly.

Bernard: But actually . . . er . . . I mean, in fact, isn't it the Minister's job to run the Department?

Sir Humphrey: No, Bernard, it is our job. To be more precise, it is my job, for which I've had twenty-five years training and practice. Don't you realize what would happen if we allowed the Minister to run the Department?

Bernard: No, what?

Sir Humphrey: First, there would be chaos, naturally. Second, and even worse – there would be innovations.

Bernard: Ah!

Sir Humphrey: Changes, Bernard.

Bernard: [*Worried*] Ooh!

Sir Humphrey: Public debate. Outside scrutiny.

Bernard: Gosh!

Sir Humphrey: Is that what you want?

Bernard: Good heavens, no. But . . . [*Puzzled*] What *should* he do then?

Sir Humphrey: A Minister has three functions. First, as an advocate, making his Department's actions seem plausible to Parliament and the public – he is, in fact, our public relations man. Second, he's our man in Westminster, steering *our* legislation through Parliament. And third, above all, he's our breadwinner – he has to fight in cabinet for the money *we* need to do *our* job. But he is emphatically *not* there to review departmental procedures with Principals and Assistant Secretaries.

Bernard: But if he's got the time –

Sir Humphrey: [*Thunderously*] *Why* has he got the time? He shouldn't have the time. That's your fault, Bernard! It is for you to ensure that he has not got the time. Create activity, Bernard! He must make speeches – provincial visits. We need deputations, junkets abroad, mountains of red boxes, crises, emergencies, panics! [*Emphatically*] *Pull yourself together, Bernard!*

[**Bernard** *tries to speak*]

Bernard: But –

Sir Humphrey: You must be leaving spaces in his diary.

Bernard: He makes them.

Sir Humphrey: Then fill them up again.

Bernard: He won't let me.

Sir Humphrey: Don't ask him. Do it. Make sure he spends more time where he's not under our feet and can't do any damage.

Bernard: Where?

Sir Humphrey: Well, the House of Commons, for instance.

Bernard: Sir Humphrey, I really am doing my best. There's a deputation in there at this moment.

Sir Humphrey: What's it about?

Bernard: Something completely trivial – preserving badgers in Warwickshire.

Sir Humphrey: [*Pleased*] Well done, Bernard. Why didn't you tell me this when I asked you before?

Bernard: Actually, I thought it was rather . . . well, trivial. Wasting the Minister's time. I thought you wouldn't approve, actually.

Sir Humphrey: [*Sadly*] Oh Bernard.

Bernard: Um, I'll try and find some other threatened species, shall I?

Sir Humphrey: [*Getting up*] You may not have to look very far, Bernard. Private Secretaries who cannot occupy their Ministers are a threatened species – actually.

2   Jim's office

A group of environmental protectionists have just finished handing over their petition to **Jim,** *who is at his desk.* **Bernard**'s *assistant is taking notes.*

Male Protester: But don't you see? We have a sacred trust to preserve our natural heritage.

Jim: Yes, well, that's what this proposed legislation is designed to achieve. As I said in the House yesterday, the present system just isn't working. It's a hotch-potch. Local authorities, tourist authorities, national parks, the countryside commission, the CPRE – nobody knows where they are, nothing gets done, and everyone is squabbling and backbiting. You know what committees are like.

Female Protester: We are a committee.

Jim: Yes, of course, I don't mean your committee. Anyway, this new set-up will create clear authority, simple procedures, and incidentally save a great deal of public money. You should welcome it.

Female Protester: That's all very well, but what about Hayward's Spinney?

Jim: Well, one or two very small areas will have to lose their protected status, because it simply isn't economic to administer them properly.

Male Protestor: But Hayward's Spinney is a vital part of Britain's heritage. The bodgers have dwelt there for generators.

Jim: How can you be sure?

Female Protester: It said so in the *Guardian*. [*She gives him a newspaper*]

Jim: [*Taking it*] Ah well . . . [*He reads the paper*] It actually says '. . . the badgers have dwelt there for generations'!

Female Protester: How would you feel if you were going to have office blocks built all over your garden by a lot of giant badgers?

Jim: But nobody is going to build office blocks . . . [*He breaks off incredulously*] Giant badgers?

Female Protester: There's nothing special about man, Mr Hacker. We're not above nature. We're all a part of it. Men are animals too, you know.

Jim: I know that. I've just come from the House of Commons.

[**Bernard** *knocks and enters*]

Bernard: Er . . . sorry to interrupt, Minister, but you're due for your next appointment.

Jim: [*With exaggerated enthusiasm*] Oh, what a pity! Well, thank you all for making your case so persuasively. It's been a great pleasure.

[**Bernard** *shepherds them towards the door*]

Bernard: You go down the corridor, turn left at the end and down the stairs.

[*The* **Female Protestor** *crosses to* **Jim** *and shakes his hand*]

Female Protester: But what are you going to do about it?

Jim: All views will be taken into consideration at the appropriate stage. Now if you'll forgive me . . .

[**Bernard** *ushers the group out and closes the door*]

Bernard: A most polished performance, Minister. Gracious. Conciliatory. And you said absolutely nothing. Very professional.

Jim: Why wasn't I warned?

Bernard: About what, Minister?

Jim: Why was I not warned that unifying the administration of the countryside would mean removing special protected status from this beaver whatsit?

Bernard: Badger colony, Minister. Hayward's Spinney, East Warwickshire.

Jim: Somebody must have known, mustn't they?

Bernard: [*Stalling*] If somebody did happen to know, Minister, they would not necessarily know that you would want to know what they happened to know, in case . . .

[*There is a knock at the door.* **Bernard** *seizes on the interruption with relief.* **Sir Humphrey** *enters*]

Bernard: Ah! Sir Humphrey!

Jim: [*Accusingly*] Humphrey!

Sir Humphrey: Good morning, Minister.

Jim: Humphrey, do you see it as your job to help ministers makes fools of themselves?

Sir Humphrey: I have never met one who needed any help. No, seriously Minister, of course that is the last thing . . .

Jim: Then why did you encourage me to stand up and tell Parliament and the press that unifying the administration of the countryside will entail no loss of amenity, when apparently I have signed a death warrant for a whole army of beavers?

Bernard: Badgers, Minister.

Jim: Badgers.

Bernard: Beavers would have a navy.

Jim: What?

Bernard: Nothing, Minister.

Jim: Well don't mutter. Humphrey, why did you let me do it?

Sir Humphrey: With respect, Minister, I did not encourage you to say that.

Jim: You did! Look at this. [*He hands him a paper*] The Department drafted this. 'No loss of amenity'.

Sir Humphrey: No, Minister. Not 'No loss of amenity', 'No *significant* loss of amenity'.

Jim: Well it's the same thing.

Sir Humphrey: On the contrary, there's all the difference in the world. Almost anything can be attacked as a loss of amenity, and almost anything can be defended as not a significant loss of amenity . . . which seems to signify that one should appreciate the significance of 'significant'.

Jim: Be that as it may, Humphrey, the publicity can still be very damaging.

Sir Humphrey: I think not, Minister.

Jim: But if I've said there's going to be no loss of amenity – and then there *is* . . .

Sir Humphrey: If you'd just like to approve this release, Minister, you'll see it counters all their arguments. [*He hands over the release, which* **Jim** *reads*] It points out that the spinney is merely deregistered, not threatened. Badgers are very plentiful all over Warwickshire. It mentions the connection between badgers and brucellosis. 'Cannot be regarded as a significant loss of amenity'. It's all there.

Jim: [*Handing it back*] So you don't think it'll make the national press?

Sir Humphrey: A few lines on an inside page of the *Guardian* perhaps, but nothing to worry about. It's only the urban middle class who worry about the preservation of the countryside, because they don't have to live in it. Anything else?

Jim: No! Yes! All right, this may blow over, but it doesn't change my basic question.

Sir Humphrey: Which was?

Jim: Why was I not told about this before I made the announcement?

Sir Humphrey: There are those who have argued – and indeed very cogently – that on occasion there are some things it is better for the Minister not to know.

Jim: [*Taking off his glasses*] Humphrey! What are you saying?

Sir Humphrey: Minister, your answers in the House and at the Press Conference were superb. You were convinced and convincing. The critics were silenced. Could you have spoken with the same authority if the ecological pressure group had been, er, badgering you?

Jim: But... but... I have a right to know! I am the people's representative! What right have you got to withhold facts from me like this? It's monstrous!

Sir Humphrey: It's in your own best interests, Minister.

Jim: What do you mean? 'Some things it is better for a Minister not to know'! It's intolerable. This must not occur again. And it so happens [*He produces a folder from his desk*] that I have a new plan here for reorganizing this Department to ensure that it doesn't.

[**Sir Humphrey** *scowls at* **Bernard,** *who looks anxious and guilty*]

Sir Humphrey: [*Coolly*] Indeed?

Jim: Yes, indeed. Now, if we had one Under-Secretary and two Assistant Secretaries reporting direct to me ...

Sir Humphrey: [*Interrupting*] Minister. Please!

Jim: Wait a minute. Let me tell you my plan.

[**Sir Humphrey** *steels himself to speak directly*]

Sir Humphrey: The plan is immaterial. Minister, I have to say something to you that you may not like to hear.

Jim: Why should today be different?

Sir Humphrey: [*Rapidly*] Minister, the traditional allocation of executive responsibilities has always been so determined as to liberate the ministerial incumbent from the administrative minutiae by devolving the managerial functions to those whose experience and qualifications have better formed them for the performance of such humble offices, thereby releasing their political overlords for the more onerous duties and profound deliberations that are the inevitable concomitant of their exalted position.

Jim: What made you think I wouldn't want to hear that?

Sir Humphrey: I thought it might upset you.

Jim: How could it? I didn't understand a word.

[**Sir Humphrey** *stares at him*]

Jim: For God's sake, Humphrey, for once in your life, put it into plain English.

Sir Humphrey: If you insist, Minister. You are not here to run this Department.

Jim: I beg your pardon?

Sir Humphrey: You are not here to run this Department.

Jim: I think I am. I think the public thinks I am, too.

Sir Humphrey: With respect, you are wrong and they are wrong.

Jim: Well, who does run this Department?

Sir Humphrey: I do.

Jim: Oh, I see ... and what am I supposed to do?

Sir Humphrey: Minister, we've been through all this before. Make policy. Get legislation enacted. And above all, secure the Department's budget in cabinet.

Jim: Sometimes I suspect that the budget is all you ever really care about.

Sir Humphrey: It is rather important. If nobody cares about the budget we could end up with a department so small that even a Minister could run it.

Jim: Humphrey, are we about to have a fundamental disagreement about the nature of democracy?

Sir Humphrey: No Minister, merely a demarcation dispute. I am only saying that the menial chore of running a department is beneath you. You were fashioned for a nobler calling.

Jim: Well, I'm quite happy to leave the routine paperwork to you – but I insist on direct access to all information. Never again do I want to hear the phrase 'There are some things it is better for a Minister not to know.' Is that clear?

Sir Humphrey: But Minister . . .

Jim: That's an order!

Sir Humphrey: As you say, Minister. If that is what you really want.

Jim: Do you think Ministers are a lot of irresponsible ten-year-olds?

[**Bernard** *laughs, and* **Jim** *reacts angrily*]

3   The kitchen of Jim's home in his constituency

Jim *and* **Annie** *are eating breakfast.* **Lucy,** *their daughter, enters. She is about eighteen, attractive but scruffy. Red boxes are piled high on a chair; one is open.*

Jim: Good-afternoon. [*Looking at his watch*]

Lucy: Have you finished with the *Guardian,* Daddy?

Jim: Yes. Sorry I haven't got a copy of the *Socialist Worker* for you.

Lucy: That's all right.

[**Annie** *tries to ease the friction between* **Jim** *and* **Lucy**]

Annie: [*Brightly*] Daddy's pleased you came down for breakfast, aren't you Jim?

[**Jim** *tries to look pleased*]

Annie: And he hasn't seen you for a while . . .

Lucy: I was having a lie-in.

Jim: Better than a sit-in. I suppose.

[**Lucy** *ignores him*]

Jim: Why were you home so late last night?

Lucy: [*Looking at him for the first time*] There are some things it is better for a father not to know.

Jim: [*Irritated*] Don't *you* start!

Annie: [*Puzzled*] What?

Jim: Nothing, nothing.

Lucy: I was out with the Trots.

Jim: [*Genuinely sympathetic*] Oh, I'm sorry. Are you going to see the Doctor about it?

Lucy: The Trotskyites!

Jim: [*Surprised*] Are you a Trotskyite now?

Lucy: No. Peter is.

Jim: Peter?

Lucy: Yes, Peter.

[**Jim** *clearly can't remember Peter.* **Lucy** *is sarcastic*]

Lucy: You've only met him about fifteen times

Jim: Oh, is he the one with the . . . [*He mimes a beard*] and the . . . [*He mimes a thick, fuzzy Afro hair-do*]

Lucy: That's right.

Annie: Jim, I need your help today.

Jim: With what?

Annie: Shopping at the cash and carry, the kitchen plughole's blocked, the lawn needs mowing . . .

Jim: Sorry, I'm busy with my boxes. They're important.

Annie: They can wait.

Jim: Annie, it may have escaped your notice that I am a Minister of the Crown. A member of Her Majesty's Government. [*With heavy irony*] I do a *fairly* important job.

Annie: But you have 23,000 civil servants to help you – I haven't. You can play with your memos later – the drains need fixing now.

[**Lucy** *stretches across* **Jim** *for some marmalade and drops it off her knife onto* **Jim**'s *papers*]

Jim: Lucy! You've got marmalade all over the Cabinet papers! [*He scrapes at it with a knife*]

Lucy: [*Unconcerned*] Sorry.

Jim: [*Impatiently*] Oh, I've got butter on them now. Get a cloth.

Lucy: Get it yourself.

Annie: Lucy.

Lucy: You're not in Whitehall now. 'Yes Minister', 'Certainly Minister', 'Just as you say, Minister', 'Please may I lick your boots, Minister?'.

[**Jim** *crosses to get a cloth*]

Annie: Lucy, darling, that's not fair. Those civil servants are always kow-towing to Daddy, but they never take any real notice of him.

Jim: I'll have you know that I just won a considerable victory at the Department. Look at that pile of boxes.

Annie: That's what I mean. For a short time you were

getting the better of Humphrey, but now they've done a snow job on you again.

Jim: No, that's not it at all. I asked for all this. [*Indicating the boxes*]

Annie: [*Stunned*] Why?

Jim: Yesterday, in so many words, Humphrey told me that there are some things that it's better for a Minister not to know. Which means he hides things from me. Who knows, important things, perhaps. [*Proudly*] So I have insisted that I'm told *everything* that goes on in the Department.

[*There is a pause*]

Annie: [*Fondly*] How did you get to be a Cabinet Minister, darling? You're such a clot.

Jim: What?

Annie: Don't you see? You've played right into Humphrey's hands. He must be utterly delighted you've given him an open invitation to swamp you with useless information.

Jim: Do you think so?

Annie: Well, what's in that box, for instance?

Jim: Um ... technical reports, feasibility studies, past papers of assorted committees, stationery requisitions ... [*He falters and looks at her.* **Annie** *reacts*] Damnation. [*He sighs*] It's Catch 22, isn't it? Either they give you so little information that you don't know the salient facts, or so much that you can't find them. [*In despair*] You can't win. They get you coming and going.

Lucy: [*Reading the newspaper*] There's a story about you here, Daddy.

Jim: [*Curtly*] I've read it.

Lucy: [*Reads the headline*] 'Hacker The Badger Butcher'.

Annie: [*Firmly*] Daddy's read it, darling.

[**Lucy** *looks at* **Jim** *beadily*]

Lucy: What's all this, then?

Jim: Load of rubbish.

Lucy: It says here 'Hacker admitted that removing protected status from Haywards Spinney could mean the end of the badger colony'. [*She eyes him, then carries on reading*] 'A spokesman for the Society for The Preservation of British Wildlife said: 'Hacker has signed the badger's death warrant'.

[**Jim** *puts his knife down, deliberately*]

Jim: One: I am not a badger butcher. Two: the badger is not an endangered species. Three: the removal of protective status does not necessarily mean the badgers will be killed. Four: if a few badgers have to be sacrificed for the sake of a master plan that will save Britain's natural heritage – tough.

Lucy: Ze master plan, mein Fuhrer. The end justifies the means, does it?

Jim: [*Wearily*] Oh Lucy, really . . .

Lucy: It's because the badgers haven't got votes, isn't it?

Jim: [*Baffled*] What?

Lucy: If badgers had votes you wouldn't be exterminating them, you'd be up there at Hayward's Spinney, shaking paws, and kissing cubs . . . ingratiating yourself the way you always do. Yugh!

Annie: Lucy, that's not a very nice thing to say.

Lucy: It's true, isn't it?

[**Annie** *reacts with reluctant acquiescence*]

Annie: Ye-e-es, it's true . . . but, well he's in politics. Daddy *has* to be ingratiating.

Jim: Thank you very much, dear.

Lucy: It's got to be stopped.

Jim: Too late. The decision's been taken.

Lucy: *I'm* going to stop it, then.

Jim: Oh fine! That should be quite easy. Just get yourself adopted as a candidate, win a general election, serve with distinction on the back benches, be appointed a Minister and repeal the Act. No problem. Of course, the badgers might be getting on a bit by then.

4   The Athenaeum Club

Sir Humphrey *and* **Sir Frederick** *are sitting in armchairs after dinner, with large glasses of brandy.*

Sir Frederick: Assistant Secretaries reporting direct to the Minister?

Sir Humphrey: I know.

Sir Frederick: What does he think he is? A civil servant? The arrogance of these politicians!

[**Bernard** *enters with some papers. The bottom document is very fat*]

Sir Humphrey: Ah, Bernard. [*He takes the papers and checks quickly*] Yes, yes, yes. Fine. [*Handing them back*] You can show the last one to the Minister if you like. Should keep him quiet for a bit. [*There is a pause*] What's the matter?

Bernard: It's just . . . I've been increasingly worried about, well, keeping things from the Minister.

Sir Frederick: Oh, shall I . . . [*He half rises*]

Sir Humphrey: No, no – [*To* **Bernard**] what do you mean?

Bernard: Well, why shouldn't he be allowed to know things if he wants to?

Sir Frederick: [*Shocked*] Silly boy!

Sir Humphrey: [*Motioning* **Bernard** *to sit down*] Bernard. This country is governed by Ministers making decisions from the various alternative proposals we offer them, is it not?

Bernard: Yes, of course.

Sir Humphrey: Well don't you see? If they had all the facts, they would see all sorts of other possibilities. They might even formulate their own plans instead of choosing between the two or three we put up.

Bernard: But would that matter?

Sir Frederick: Would it matter!

Bernard: Why?

Sir Humphrey: Bernard. As long as we are the ones who formulate the proposals, we can, er, guide them to the correct decision.

Bernard: Can we? How?

[**Sir Humphrey** *and* **Sir Frederick** *exchange glances, showing they agree that* **Bernard** *can be told. There is a pause*]

Sir Frederick: It's like a conjuror. 'The Three Card Trick'. You know, 'Take any card' and then make sure they take the one you intend. Ours is the Four Word Trick.

[**Bernard** *looks blankly at* **Sir Humphrey**]

Sir Humphrey: There are four words you have to work into a proposal if you want the Minister to accept it.

Sir Frederick: 'Simple'. 'Quick'. 'Popular'. 'Cheap'. And equally, four words to work into a proposal if you want it thrown out.

Sir Humphrey: 'Complicated'. 'Lengthy'. 'Expensive'. 'Controversial'. And if you really want to make sure the Minister doesn't accept it, say the decision would be courageous.

Bernard: Is that worse than 'controversial'?

Sir Humphrey: Oh yes. 'Controversial' only means 'This will lose you votes.' 'Courageous' means 'This will lose you the election.'

Sir Frederick: But if they have all the facts, instead of just the options – they might start to think for themselves!

Bernard: And the system works?

Sir Humphrey: Works? It's made Britain what she is today.

Bernard: Oh yes. I see.

Sir Frederick: So what are you going to do about your man, Humpy?

Sir Humphrey: Well, I'm giving him plenty to read.

Sir Frederick: Shouldn't you look for an opportunity to show him the positive virtues of being kept in ignorance?

Sir Humphrey: Well if he doesn't know that after twenty years as a politican . . .

[*They laugh and look at* **Bernard,** *who is unsure whether or not to join in*]

5   Jim's office

Red boxes are on the desk, one of them is open. **Bernard** *takes a file from the box and then notices an envelope in the bottom of the box. He picks it up, puzzled.*
   Sir Humphrey *enters.*

Sir Humphrey: You look worried, Bernard.

Bernard: Yes, Sir Humphrey. It's this letter. I found it in one of the Minister's boxes.

Sir Humphrey: What about it?

Bernard: I don't know whether to open it or not?

Sir Humphrey: You know the rules. Private secretaries open every classification up to and including Top Secret. Only letters marked 'personal' shall remain unopened, unless the Minister orders otherwise.

Bernard: What about 'Daddy'?

Sir Humphrey: [*Puzzled*] I do not immediately see where your father comes into this.

Bernard: No, no. It's addressed to 'Daddy'. 'Urgent'.

Sir Humphrey: Does it say 'Personal'?

Bernard: No.

Sir Humphrey: You know the rules – it must be opened.

[**Bernard** *opens the letter*]

Bernard: It's from the Minister's daughter.

Sir Humphrey: You astound me, Bernard.

[**Bernard** *continues reading*]

Bernard: Oh. [*Reading*] Oh dear . . . oh dear . . . oh dear!

Sir Humphrey: Trouble at the mill?

Bernard: Miss Hacker intends to join the badger protest.

Sir Humphrey: I thought it was over.

Bernard: She and her boyfriend are going to conduct a 24-hour 'Save-the badgers' vigil in Hayward's Spinney unless the protection order is restored. And they are putting their announcement out to the press at 5.00 pm.

Sir Humphrey: I see. 'Minster's daughter in badger protest vigil'. Well, I suppose it is a little embarrassing, but not too serious.

Bernard: I think, Sir Humphrey, the Minister may find it more than a little embarrassing.

Sir Humphrey: What do you mean?

Bernard: 'Minister's daughter in *nude* badger protest vigil'.

Sir Humphrey: [*Astounded*] What?

Bernard: Miss Hacker and her boyfriend will be . . . that is, will not be . . . [*He gestures miserably*]

Sir Humphrey: Starkers, Bernard?

Bernard: Yes, Sir Humphrey.

Sir Humphrey: Ah. That puts a different complexion on it.

Bernard: Especially in this weather.

Sir Humphrey: [*Taking the letter and looking at it*] To put in crude journalistic terms, this makes it a big story. Front page . . . with photograph.

[**Jim** *enters.* **Sir Humphrey** *and* **Bernard** *rise, and turn to face* **Jim**]

Jim: Hallo, Humphrey.

[*There is a pause.* **Jim** *looks from* **Sir Humphrey** *to* **Bernard** *and back*]

Jim: Anything wrong? [*Another pause*] Well?

Sir Humphrey: Shall we say a slight embarrassment, Minister?

Jim: How slight?

Sir Humphrey: Well, while not in any sense wishing to overstate the case or suggest there might be cause for undue alarm, nevertheless, the fact remains, er . . .

Jim: For heaven's sake, Humphrey! Out with it!

Sir Humphrey: Minister, I have a confession to make.

Jim: That's a change. [*He waits*] Well come on, make a clean breast of it.

Sir Humphrey: Not the happiest of phrases in the circumstances, Minister.

Jim: What do you mean?

Sir Humphrey: I have to confess that the badgers in Hayward's Spinney may turn out to be a somewhat bigger story than we thought.

Jim: Why? Are they going to have kittens or something?

Sir Humphrey: It is not the *badgers* who are going to have kittens, Minister. There is going to be a 24-hour protest vigil in Hayward's Spinney.

Jim: So? You told me it wouldn't be very newsworthy.

Sir Humphrey: I'm afraid this is rather different. It is being conducted by . . . by . . . by a girl student and her boyfriend.

Jim: Just two people?

Sir Humphrey: Yes.

Jim: Well, they don't matter, do they? A couple of irresponsible layabouts.

Bernard: They might matter to some people, Minister.

Bernard: Nonsense, Bernard. Everyone's fed up with all these ghastly students. They're just exhibitionists, you know.

Sir Humphrey: In this case they seem to have something to exhibit.

Jim: What do you mean?

Sir Humphrey: It is to be a nude protest vigil.

[*There is a long pause*]

Jim: But that will be all over the front pages!

Sir Humphrey: Quite so.

Jim: The press mustn't find out.

[**Sir Humphrey** *looks at him*]

Jim: Really, I don't know what gets into these students. Appalling. Quite shameless.

Sir Humphrey: Indeed, Minister.

Jim: It's their parents, you know.

[**Sir Humphrey** *looks inquiringly*]

Jim: Don't bring them up properly. Let them run wild, and feed them all this trendy middle-class anti-establishment nonsense.

Sir Humphrey: I'm sure it's not entirely their parent's fault, Minister?

Jim: Of course it is ... Authority, Humphrey. All this student anarchy is a shocking indictment of their parent's lack of authority and discipline. So they take it out on innocent people like me. Who are they anyway?

Sir Humphrey: We know the young lady's name.

Jim: Lady? Hah! Who is she?

Sir Humphrey: It seems she is a Miss Hacker.

Jim: Hacker ... that's my name. That's a coincidence.

Sir Humphrey: Not a complete coincidence, Minister.

Jim: You don't mean ... not Lucy?

[**Sir Humphrey** *hands him the letter*]

Jim: Oh my God ... oh my God.

Sir Humphrey: As you see, Minister, she is telephoning in ten minutes time ...

Jim: Perhaps the press ... won't be all that interested ...?

[**Sir Humphrey** *gazes at him*]

Jim: They will be, won't they?

[**Sir Humphrey** *nods*]

Jim: But will they really think it's worth going all the way to Warwickshire?

Sir Humphrey: For a story like this, Minister, I fear they would think it worth going all the way to the South Pole.

Jim: How can we kill the story? Advise me, Humphrey ...

Sir Humphrey: What about a bit of parental authority and discipline?

Jim: Don't be silly, Humphrey.

Bernard: If you could make her listen to reason ...

Jim: She's a sociology student, Bernard!

Sir Humphrey: Perhaps Mrs Hacker could lock her in her room?

Jim: Annie's out at work. [*He pauses*] What about the police?

Sir Humphrey: 'Minister sets police on nude daughter'? I'm not sure that completely kills the story, Minister.

Jim: There must be something we can do.

[*There is a slight pause.* **Sir Humphrey** *speaks hopefully*]

Sir Humphrey: Perhaps if I looked at the files?

Jim: Oh, marvellous! My daughter's about to get herself all over the front page of the *Sun*, and probably page three as well, and all you can think of is the files. Brilliant!

Sir Humphrey: Nevertheless . . .

Bernard: [*Pointing to his own office*] They're all out there, Sir Humphrey.

[**Sir Humphrey** *exits to* **Bernard's** *office*]

Jim: I wonder what sort of angle they'll take.

Bernard: Wide angle, I should think . . .

[**Jim** *reacts angrily*]

Bernard: Oh, I see what you mean, Minister.

Jim: Just think of the fun the Opposition will have with this. 'Does the proud Father want to make a statement?' 'Is the Minister's family getting too much exposure?' 'Did the Minister try to conduct a cover-up?'

Bernard: 'Does the Minister run the Department any better than he runs his family?'

Jim: [*Ruefully*] And I suppose you'll want me to tell them that Humphrey runs it, won't you?

Bernard: [*Shocked*] No, Minister, not I! I am your Private Secretary.

Jim: [*Disbelievingly*] You mean, when the chips are down, you'll be on my side, not Humphrey's?

Bernard: Minister, it is my job to see that the chips stay up.

[*The phone buzzes –* **Jim** *and* **Bernard** *stare transfixed; it buzzes again – they stare at each other; it buzzes a third time –* **Bernard** *picks up the receiver*]

Bernard: Hallo . . .

6   A telephone conversation

Lucy *is phoning from a telephone kiosk with* **Peter,** *her student boyfriend. He is equally unkempt, has thick specs and an Afro hairstyle, and is clearly dominated by* **Lucy.** *At the other end of the line we see* **Jim** *at his desk, with* **Sir Humphrey** *and* **Bernard** *also in* **Jim**'s *office.* **Peter** *remains completely deadpan throughout the scene and never visibly responds to anything that is said.*

Lucy: Can I speak to Mr Hacker, please? It's his daughter.

Bernard: [*Handing the phone to* **Jim**] I think this is for you, Minister.

Jim: Ah, Lucy. Hallo, darling.

Lucy: [*Without emotion*]Hallo, Daddy.

Jim: I, er, I got your little note. [*He laughs falsely*] You know for a moment I was taken in. I thought it was serious.

Lucy: It is serious. It's deadly serious, isn't it, Pete? [**Peter** *is deadpan*] Pete and I are just going to ring Exchange Telegraph and the Press Association, then we're off to the Spinney.

Jim: But darling, you can't. Think of the damage.

Lucy: What damage?

Jim: Well . . . to me.

Lucy: Damage to you? Isn't that typical? [**Peter** *is deadpan*] What about damage to badgers? It's not you who's going to be exterminated, is it?

Jim: Well . . . in a sense, yes.

Lucy: OK. Then you know what to do.

Jim: Look, Lucy, hold on . . .

Lucy: Ten. Nine. Eight . . .

[*She is counting fairly slowly and deliberately*]

Jim: Lucy!

[**Lucy's** *countdown continues;* **Sir Humphrey** *enters with a file*]

Sir Humphrey: A moment, Minister. Could I have a word with the lady?

Jim: Lucy! Sir Humphrey Appleby would like a word with you.

Sir Humphrey: A new development.

Jim: A new development.

Lucy: Six . . . five . . .

[**Sir Humphrey** *takes the phone*]

Sir Humphrey: Miss Hacker . . . ah, how do you do? I'm Sir Humphrey Appleby, Mr Hacker's Permanent Secretary.

Lucy: Five and holding.

Sir Humphrey: Yes . . . if I might have a word, dear lady. I have just come upon the latest report from the Government's own wildlife inspectors. It throws a new light on the issue.

Lucy: [*Impatiently*] Why?

Sir Humphrey: Apparently there is no badger colony in Hayward's Spinney. It says '. . . last evidence of badger habitation – droppings, freshly turned earth, etc. – was recorded eleven years ago'.

Lucy: But the papers said . . .

Sir Humphrey: Quite so. Apparently the story was fed to them by a local property developer.

Lucy: Property developer?

Sir Humphrey: Yes. You see the local authority have plans to use the spinney for a new College of Further Education, but the developer wants to buy it for offices and luxury flats.

Lucy: But if it's protected he won't be able to.

Sir Humphrey: Ah, but nor will the council. And he knows that if they can't, they'll spend the money on something else. Then he can move in, in twelve months time, show that there's no badger colony, get protection removed and build his offices. It's quite common practice.

Lucy: So you mean there isn't actually any wildlife in the spinney at all?

Sir Humphrey: There is some. It's been used as a rubbish dump by people from Birmingham, so there are lots of rats.

Lucy: [*She swallows – she is terrified of rats*] Rats?

Sir Humphrey: Yes. Thousands of them, apparently. Though I suppose they are wildlife too, in their way. [*He pauses*] But it would be a pity to play into the developer's hands, wouldn't it?

Lucy: I suppose it would.

Sir Humphrey: But do let me say how much I respect your views and commitment. Do you want to speak to the Minister again?

Lucy: No, that's all right. Oh well. Forget it, then.

[*She rings off, turns to* **Peter** *and shrugs*]

7   Jim's office

Jim: Humphrey! I take it all back!

Sir Humphrey: It was nothing, Minister. It was all in the files.

Jim: A property developer? God, the cunning devils . . . can I see that report?

Sir Humphrey: [*Evasively*] It's not very interesting, really.

Jim: No, come on, let's see it.

Sir Humphrey: Quite honestly, I don't think you'd . . .

Jim: [*With sudden suspicion*] Humphrey! It was true, wasn't it? [*Pause*] Humphrey, was there one word of truth in that whole story you told Lucy?

Sir Humphrey: Do you really want me to answer that question, Minister?

[*There is a long pause*]

Jim: [*Firmly*] No, Humphrey, I don't think I do.

Sir Humphrey: Quite so. Perhaps there are some things it is better for a Minister not to know.

[**Jim** *sits back resignedly, and* **Sir Humphrey** *smiles confidently*]

Follow-up Activities

Open All Hours

Discussion points
1 Whose side do we take in the scenes between Arkwright and Granville? And whose side in the scenes between Arkwright and his customers? Why is this? Which characters do you find likeable?
2 In this episode, who 'wins'? That is, who comes off best in the end?
3 Would *Open All Hours* be just as funny if Arkwright did not stutter? Is the script making fun of people who stutter?
4 Do the scenes between Arkwright and Nurse Gladys make fun of Nurse Gladys (and treat her simply as a sex object) or do they make fun of Arkwright? Do they offend you in any way?
5 How realistic is the script, do you think?

Activities
1 Suppose that Granville keeps a diary. Write his entry for the day on which scenes 1–11 take place.
2 Improvise (or write in script form) a scene in which Mrs Blewitt and Mavis meet and discuss Arkwright after their visits to his shop.
3 Various types of humour can be found in *Open All Hours*.

For example, there are examples of slapstick or visual humour, puns, *double entendres*, 'stock routines' (that is, 'regular' or recurring jokes, like the business with the till), etc. Make separate lists of these. Which are the most frequent? What other types of humour can you find in the script? Which kinds of joke or humour do you prefer?

4   In pairs, improvise (or write) a scene involving a shop assistant and a customer who has trouble making up his or her mind about what to buy. You could perhaps set it in either a shoe shop or post office. The assistant (who is worried about losing his or her job) should struggle to remain as polite as possible.

5   Improvise or write a scene between the manager or manageress of the clothing department of a large store and an assistant. By mistake, the manager has ordered far too many items of a particular line and wants the assistant to make sure as many as possible are sold. (You might try tape-recording this or any other of your improvisations and later turn them into written scripts. You will probably find you can improve them by rewriting parts to make them funnier and by editing out the weaker parts).

6   If you have ever had a part-time job in a shop, write about your experiences.

7   Suppose you work on a till in a supermarket. Work out what is the best order in which to perform the following tasks when serving a customer:
   (a) pressing 'total' key to open till drawer
   (b) counting out change into your own hand
   (c) checking condition of goods
   (d) placing customer's money in till drawer
   (e) closing till drawer
   (f) thanking the customer
   (g) keying in the prices of each item
   (h) receiving money from customer

(i)   counting change into customer's hand
(j)   tearing off till receipt and giving it to customer
(k)   wrapping any goods that need wrapping
Now write a notice giving instructions to trainee till operators on how to serve a customer.

8   Suppose you get a part-time job in Arkwright's shop. While pricing bottles of cooking oil, you drop one and oil spills onto the floor. Write a short story about the accident and what happened.

Only When I Laugh

Discussion points

1   With which character or characters is the viewer expected to identify? That is, on whose side is the viewer expected to be? Whose side do you take? How does the author make you take sides?

2   What do you find realistic and unrealistic about this episode? If any of it does strike you as being unrealistic or improbable, do you find this spoils your enjoyment of it?

3   Why do you think many people want to be on television (or want to be seen on television), even if only in a crowd?

4   What would happen if a television film crew tried to make a film about a day in the life of your school? Do you think it is possible for television to show things as they really are?

5   When you are watching television, can you tell fact from fiction? How?

Activities

1   Imagine that Figgis, Glover and Norman each wrote a letter to a friend or relative about the television crew's visit to the hospital. Write each of those letters,

describing what happened from each of their points of view to show how they each see the day's events.

2   Suppose Gary and Phil return to their television company with very little usable film. They must write a report for the editor of the programme on which they work, describing as briefly and factually as possible what happened and why the day was wasted. Write their report.

3   Suppose the film crew had come to the same hospital to make a programme about a day in the life of a patient. Using the same characters as appear in *Only When I Laugh* plan and then improvise or write two or three scenes for such an episode.

4   Write about a time when you have been in hospital or have visited someone who was in hospital. (This need not be a comic story, of course.)

5   Watch an early evening news magazine programme on television. List each item and note the member of the public (i.e. non-television performers) who appear. How must being on that programme have altered their day? Will they have been pleased to have been on the programme?

6   In groups, plan a documentary about school. It could, for example, be a film about a day in the life of a school caretaker. Limit the number of interviews to three or four and plan carefully the order of other scenes that should be filmed and their locations. When you have a 'running order' or list of the 'shots' (including any general ones to show the viewer where it is all happening), begin improvising your documentary. Later you might actually be able to make a short 8mm film or videotape documentary about a similar subject.

Hancock's Half Hour

Discussion points

1   In some situation comedies, all the characters are meant to be comic. In others, there are several who are meant to be comic while others are serious or 'straight'. Which are the comic ones in this script?

2   In some of his shows, Tony Hancock was presented as almost a tragic character: you often felt sorry for him, even while you were laughing at him. Do you ever feel sorry for him in this episode?

3   'Soap opera' began in the United States of America. Daily serials were broadcast on radio to advertise different products, especially soap powders – hence the nickname. Why do you think television and radio soap operas are so popular? Which do you like best? Are there any you really dislike? What is it about them that you dislike?

4   The BBC radio soap opera, *The Archers*, began in 1950. When Independent Television began in 1955, a special event was planned to take place in *The Archers* just before Independent Television started broadcasting, in order to distract publicity from the new channel.

The death of Grace, in a stable blaze while she was trying to rescue her horse, was timed to perfection – only minutes before the new channel was opened on the evening of Thursday, 23 September. The result was that it was *The Archers* that got massive coverage in the press the next day. 'Radio fans wept as Grace Archer "died" (*Daily Mirror*); 'Archer fans upset when Grace dies' (*News Chronicle*); 'Why do this to Grace Archer?' (*Daily Express*); 'Millions shocked as Grace dies' (*Daily Herald*); 'Death of BBC serial character' (*The Times*); 'Why Grace Archer died' (*Daily Mail*); 'Listeners sob as Grace Archer "dies" (*Daily Sketch*); 'Upset by "death" in the Archers' (*Daily Telegraph*) . . .

In the days that followed, the BBC estimated that some

15,000 letters of protest were received – it was impossible to count the number of telephone calls – and a pair of coffin-handles and brass plates were delivered to the Birmingham studios. For fear that they would be inundated with flowers, it was decided that the 'funeral' would not be held within the programme.

Do you think excessive interest and even belief in soap operas is dangerous?

5   The 'death' of Grace Archer was planned carefully at a meeting between the script writers and producer:

Grace should die after a miscarriage, said someone. No, no, that would upset every expectant mother in the land. Grace should die in a road accident. No, that would frighten everybody whose wife was out in her car at the time. How about her dying in a stable fire, then? Yes, that was it – and if she first escaped the flames and then rushed back into the blazing stables to try to save her horse, would not that be a fitting end for a heroine?

But a writer cannot just decide he or she will kill off any character:

An Archers writer has the freedom to do anything – anything, that is, except kill characters off.

That sort of decision is reserved for meetings in a pleasant Cotswold hotel. Every six months or so the writers meet there, and over afternoon tea and cream cakes, gentle voices can be heard murmuring . . .
'Ralph Bellamy's always moaning about having a heart attack, let's give him one . . .'
'Perhaps we could kill Lizzie Larkin off in a car crash . . .'
But writers are not naturally vicious or bloodthirsty. There is a marked reluctance to get rid of anybody. Every character has a following among the public, and deaths are a messy business and generally bad for trade. Younger listeners might accept the demise of a central character with equanimity, but older listeners are not cheered. No, characters are only moved or killed out of necessity. Some have to go to make room for new characters (the budget only allows for the casting of a limited

number of people each week) and others go because the actor or actress wants to leave, and re-casting is not considered practicable.

How would you 'write out' a particular character in a soap opera you know? (You must not offend your viewers or listeners.)

Activities

1   Imagine *The Bowmans* was a real radio series and that the two episodes 'recorded' in this *Hancock* script have been transmitted. Write a letter to a newspaper expressing your feelings about what happens in the series.

2   As a group activity, select the 'best' or most interesting parts of these letters and compile a newspaper letters column from them.

3   Choose a soap opera that you know well. Watch an episode and then plot or plan what will happen to each group of characters next, using all the clues you can find in the episodes you have watched. Try to write the next episode's script before you watch it again. Remember that each episode needs to end with at least one of its storylines at a 'cliff-hanging' stage to tempt the viewers to watch again. Remember too that viewers like characters in soap operas to behave 'in character' – that is, not to do anything untypical.

4   The following is a description of how *Coronation Street* is planned:

Every three weeks a story conference is convened to make decisions about the narrative progression of a further six episodes, within the broader framework of a long-term conference held periodically to map out future directions. In attendance at the story conference are the producer, the series planner, the storyline writers and a number of script writers. Plot developments for a three-week period are discussed and proceedings and decisions minuted. The storyline writers then produce the outlines of six episodes based on the decisions of the conference, and these are allocated to suitable writers.

In groups, plan your own soap opera. Begin by deciding its location (e.g. a school, cafe, shop or other place of work) and then decide on the main eight or ten characters. Plan a number of storylines, each of which will run through several episodes. Try writing or improvising a number of scenes from it.

5   Suppose Tony Hancock was given a part (of an additional character) in a serial you watch. Write a description of a rehearsal.

6   Suppose this edition of *Hancock's Half Hour* was going to be repeated. As a television critic, would you encourage the readers of your newspaper to watch it or not? Write a 200-word article (called 'Tonight on Television') for an evening paper, in which you 'preview' the programme, giving your view of it.

7   Debate the motion that television plays too large a part in our lives today.

8   Collect together newspaper cuttings about events 'behind the scenes' of television programmes. How do newspapers report the real-life stories of television actors and performers? Is such reporting fair? Is too much attention paid to such 'stars'?

A Fine Romance

Discussion points

1   Which is your favourite character? Why?

2   Are Phil and Helen kind in trying to bring Mike and Laura together?

3   Do you think Mike and Laura could be happy together?

4   What do you dread about being forty-three? In what sort of situation do you hope you will *not* be at that age?

5   Do you think it is possible to help really shy people? How?

6   How does *A Fine Romance* differ from many situation comedies?

Activities

1   Improvise or write a scene in which Phil and Helen discuss the evening as they wash up after the party.

2   Write (and perform) telephone conversations that might take place next morning between (a) Helen and Laura and (b) Phil and Mike. NB No one is to say anything that is untrue in either conversation.

3   Improvise a party. Before starting, decide who will be the hosts. Each guest (or couple of guests) must decide who they are and what sort of character they are, their jobs, interests and hobbies, etc. At the party, try to find out as much as possible about as many other guests as possible.

4   Write a short story about two shy teenagers, neither of whom is very keen on the other, but who decide to pretend they are interested in each other in order to impress and satisfy their friends.

5   Write a poem expressing the feelings of a shy person at a party.

6   Plan a stage production of this episode of *A Fine Romance*. Which scenes would be difficult to present on stage? How could they be adapted so that they could be presented easily without involving a lot of scenery changes? After adapting it, rehearse and present it. (*Note:* the script is copyright and permission must be sought before any performance is given to an invited or paying audience.)

Yes Minister

Discussion points

1   Who, if anyone, 'wins' this episode? Explain how the victory is achieved.
2   Which characters do you like or admire?
3   Discuss which political party you think Jim Hacker belongs to.
4   Why does Sir Humphrey 'need' Hacker?
5   If it was your decision, would you ever allow an important area of natural beauty to be used for new housing? Is conservation of the countryside important?
6   Would it matter if a colony of badgers was 'lost'? Is conservation of wildlife important?
7   What sort of demonstrations are effective? Can they change public opinion?
8   Is a free press important?
9   Why do you think this series has proved so popular?
10 Suppose you were the editor of a newspaper. Can you think of any news item you would agree not to print if you were asked not to? For example, if the story was about a politician? Or if it was a story about a family and would cause them distress if it appeared.

Activities

1   Improvise or script the scene that might have taken place in the Hacker household at breakfast time the morning after Lucy has called off her protest.
2   The authors of *Yes Minister* have rewritten the scripts in book form, as though they were the published diaries of Jim Hacker. This is his 'entry' for the day he met the environmental committee (scene 2):

Today I had an environmental issue to deal with. A deputation of several environmentalists brought me a petition. Six fat exercise books, full of signatures. There must be thousands of signatures, if not hundreds of thousands.

They were protesting about my proposed new legislation to sort out all the existing confusions and anomalies in the present system – not that you can call it a system – which is a mess, a hotchpotch. Local authorities, tourist authorities, national parks, the National Trust, the Countryside Commission, the CPRE are all backbiting and buckpassing and nobody knows where they are and nothing gets done. The sole purpose of the new legislation is to tidy all this up and make all these wretched committees work together.

I explained this to the deputation. 'You know what committees are?' I said. 'Always squabbling and procrastinating and wasting everyone's time.'

'We are a committee.' said one of them . . . She seemed rather offended.

Try writing his entries for (a) his Saturday morning at home (scene 3) and (b) the day of Lucy's phone call.

3   Suppose Lucy's protest had gone ahead. How do you think, one of the 'serious' newspapers (e.g. the *Guardian*) would have reported it? And how do you think one of the 'popular' newspapers (e.g. the *Daily Mail*) would have reported it?

4   Plan and improvise a television news report about the threatened badger colony in Warwickshire (such as might have been transmitted before Lucy's threatened protest).

5   Sir Humphrey and Sir Frederick talk about the ways in which words can be used to get a Minister to do what they want him to do (scene 4). Suppose there was a debate in your school about whether to introduce (or abolish) a school uniform. Write two letters which might be sent to all the parents, one being worded to make them think it is a good idea to change the present situation, the other worded so as to keep things as they are.

6   Debate the motion: 'All politicians are selfish.'

7   Plan and write a 'trailer' for this edition of *Yes Minister*

which would be suitable for transmission the night before the programme was due to be shown, and which would make viewers want to watch the programme; or write the 'blurb' for the programme which would appear in the *Radio Times*. Try to make your readers want to watch the programme.

8   Imagine you are the council who has to decide what to do with the land. One group of the council members should be the conservationists, who want to keep the land free for badgers. One group should support the property developers who want to build on the land. One group should support a Ramblers' Association who feel it is important to have space to walk on. One group should be keen to use the land to build more houses for the homeless. Debate the issue and then vote. Who gets the land?

9   Collect together a number of newspaper reports of speeches by Members of Parliament and Ministers. Do you think they would be pleased by the way they have been reported? How might they have preferred to be reported? Rewrite the reports so that they are either more critical or more favourable. Compare different newspaper reports of the same speech.

General discussion points

1   Which situation comedies now being transmitted do you like best? Why? Which ones do you find boring or unfunny? Why?

2   Why do you think the shows represented in this book proved popular on television?

3   Sometimes people describe humour as being either 'coarse' or 'sophisticated'. What do they mean by such labels? What other labels could be applied to each of the scripts in this collection?

4   How do class divisions and class consciousness figure in situation comedy?

5   Are any subjects or situations unsuitable for a comedy series? Should comedy be censored? What makes a 'good' joke?

6   Is laughter cruel? How can it be uplifting or liberating? How can it be used as a weapon?

7   Do you like watching new comedy series or do you prefer ones you know?

8   Do you like a situation comedy to be realistic? Which of the shows in this book do you find most authentic or true-to-life? Which do you like best? Why?

9   Do you agree with this judgement of comedy shows (by Barry Took):

> They don't have to teach, or enhance our lives, or help us towards perfection. They merely have to help us pass thirty minutes or so in a pleasurable way, in order that we forget for a moment the real and pressing problems of our lives.

10   Why do you think people tell jokes about minorities like gays or make sexist jokes about women? To many people such jokes are offensive. In what ways are they also harmful?

11   In 1982, the Commission for Racial Equality published a report called Television in a Multi-Racial Society. Some of its findings were summarised in the magazine *Broadcast*:

> The report cites several examples of how black and Asian people were treated on screen. Programmes like Thames Television's *Love Thy Neighbour*, BBC's *Till Death Us Do Part*, LWT's *Curry and Chips* and *Mind Your Language* portrayed ethnic minorities negatively.

Do you think any series currently being shown on television contains racist jokes?

12   What can comedy achieve? Do situation comedies reinforce prejudice?

Projects

1   With the help of *Radio Times* and *TV Times*, make a list of situation comedies transmitted on the various television channels over the course of a month. What are their recurring subjects and themes? Why do you think they are scheduled at the times they are?

2   Select one of the scripts in this collection. Imagine you are directing it for television. What studio settings would you need? Would filming on location be necessary? What characteristics will you be looking for in the actors and actresses who might play the minor roles?

3   Watch a situation comedy being transmitted currently. What sort of comedy does it contain? Which 'jokes' get the biggest (or longest) laughs?

4   Collect together a number of reviews of a comedy show you have seen recently. Which do you think are fair?

5   Try planning a new situation comedy. What would make a good situation? Who would be the regular characters? What might be possible storylines?

6   Adapt part of one of the television scripts in this book for radio. Remember: none of the action can be seen. You must rely entirely on sound effects and on dialogue. You will obviously have to write additional dialogue so that the audience knows what is happening, but try to avoid unreal lines that people would never say. For example, it would be better to establish a scene with a line like, 'I like watching the river from up here,' rather than with one like, 'Here we are then, on the bridge.'